HEALTH CARE ISSUES, COSTS AND ACCESS

HOSPICE CARE

HEALTH SERVICES, QUALITY AND CLINICAL MANAGEMENT

HEALTH CARE ISSUES, COSTS AND ACCESS

Additional books in this series can be found on Nova's website under the Series tab.

Additional e-books in this series can be found on Nova's website under the e-book tab.

HEALTH CARE ISSUES, COSTS AND ACCESS

HOSPICE CARE

HEALTH SERVICES, QUALITY AND CLINICAL MANAGEMENT

JURGEN HANL
AND
SEBASTIAN KOECK
EDITORS

New York

Library of Congress Cataloging-in-Publication Data

ISBN: 978-1-62618-456-5

Library of Congress Control Number: 2013935082

Published by Nova Science Publishers, Inc. † New York

Contents

Preface **vii**

Chapter 1 Providing Hospice Care to Lesbian, Gay, Bisexual and Transgender (LGBT) Populations **1**
Finn C. G. Reygan and Paul D'Alton

Chapter 2 Sociological Explanations for the Quality of End-of-Life Care in Finland **23**
James M. Hoefler

Chapter 3 Renal Considerations in Palliative Medicine **45**
Thomas Bui

Chapter 4 Using Evidence-based Measures to Document Decline in Hospice Patients: Regulation Meets Clinical Practice **61**
William D. Cabin and Susan Havens Lang

Chapter 5 Implementation of Hospice and Palliative Medicine Training in the United States to Meet Patients' End-of-Life Needs **81**
Thomas Bui

Chapter 6 Bridging the Gap in End-of-Life Care Decision Making **93**
Alaina J. Brown and Teresa P. Díaz-Montes

Chapter 7 Ethical Issues in Hospice **103**
Padmashri Rastogi

Index **109**

PREFACE

In this book, the authors present current research in the study of the health services, quality and clinical management issues relating to hospice care. Topics discussed in this compilation include the sociological explanations for quality of end-of-life care in Finland; providing hospice care to lesbian, gay, bisexual and transgender (LGBT) populations; renal considerations in palliative medicine; using evidence-based measures to document the decline in hospice patients; implementation of hospice and palliative medicine training in the United States to meet patients' end-of-life needs; bridging the gap in end-of-life care decision making; and the ethical issues in hospice care.

Chapter 1 – There is a growing research focus internationally on the healthcare needs of lesbian, gay, bisexual and transgender (LGBT) populations including in hospices and in palliative and end-of-life (EOL) care. Nevertheless LGBT patients too often remain invisible to healthcare providers who generally receive little or no training on the healthcare needs of these populations. Training lacunae and lack of LGBT cultural competencies have been shown to detrimentally affect the quality of care provided to LGBT patients in varied healthcare settings, including in palliative and EOL care. In contrast, a growing number of professional bodies in the health sciences internationally are developing guidelines for healthcare providers on providing optimally managed care to LGBT populations. These guidelines require that healthcare providers become aware of the specific clinical issues as well as the socio-cultural and legal issues involved in providing care to LGBT people. In contrast to the general dearth of training in the area, a number of models of good practice with LGBT populations have been developed internationally. In this chapter the authors focus on one example which is work they developed in Ireland which prepares multidisciplinary healthcare teams to provide culturally sensitive and optimal palliative and EOL care to LGBT populations. This training module was developed on the premise that cross-cultural clinical competencies are increasingly being understood to include the healthcare needs of LGBT populations. Therefore this chapter outlines recent, evidence based research on the clinical needs of LGBT populations receiving palliative and EOL care; contextualises the personal histories and current socio-cultural concerns of LGBT populations; presents examples of good international practice in providing optimal care to LGBT populations; and offers recommendations for the inclusion of sexual and gender diversity into training programmes in the health sciences, specifically in hospice programmes.

Chapter 2 – Tremendous strides have been made in the last two decades with regard to the quality of palliative care available to patients at the end of life. But progress has not been uniform across the countries of western and northern Europe. Despite its well-earned reputation as one of the generally progressive welfare states of greater Scandinavia, Finland (like its Nordic neighbours) tends to trail behind other western European countries when it comes to end-of-life care policies and practices. A comparative analysis of recent research on palliative care at the end of life, together with research on sociological perspectives related to the care of the dying in western Europe, suggests that cultural forces underlie the generally lower quality of end-of-life care in Scandinavia. At the same time, there is evidence to suggest that Finland is generally well positioned to make advances in end-of-life care.

Chapter 3 – Palliative evaluation and interventions for End Stage Renal Disease (ESRD) are often not systematically implemented for the 400,000 people in the United States on dialysis, which nonetheless maintains a mortality rate of 15 to 20% per year. A significant public health and Medicare policy concern, treating ESRD patients directly costs the United States over $40 billion in public and private funds annually. Although dialysis is life sustaining, patient-physician relationships that emphasize shared decision-making on rational dialysis will maximize quality of life. Patient-centered decisions for the ESRD population, typically on dialysis as destination therapy, must primarily ask whether a patient agrees to the quality of life ramifications of initiating dialysis. Validated prognostic tools, such as the Charleson Comorbidity Index and National Kidney Foundation guidelines, assist patients prioritizing their treatment preferences. Then palliative services must be offered to all ESRD patients who suffer burdens of disease. ESRD standard of care must implement palliative best practices for treatment of uremic pruritis, neuropathy, depression, protein-energy malnutrition, and renal considerations of opioid-based pain management. Rational dialysis – not rationing dialysis – prescribes an organized plan for the ESRD patient and family to individualize risks and benefits of starting and/or withdrawing dialysis with appropriate hospice support. Using a systematic approach to communicate about diagnosis, prognosis, treatment options, and goals of care is a realistic patient advocacy strategy and restores ESRD patients' dignity at the end of life.

Chapter 4 – Hospices have been implementing various approaches to cope with the increased regulatory scrutiny in the last five years, prompted by concern about costs and outcomes. Medicare has increased demands on hospices: enacting more demanding participation criteria in 2008; new mandatory quality data collection and public reporting requirements beginning in 2012; and, through its fiscal intermediaries, more restrictive Local coverage determination (LCD) guidelines for initial and ongoing patient eligibility criteria. This chapter examines how one New York State hospice, ABC hospice, designed a multi-faceted program to simultaneously improve regulatory compliance and improve patient quality of life (QOL). This chapter presents how evidence-based scales in four patient outcome areas (i.e., pain, breathing, functional decline, and anxiety) were developed, implemented and the preliminary evaluation of results. The chapter helps inform hospices implementing public reporting and other regulatory compliance coping strategies consistent with appropriate clinical practice.

Chapter 5 – Effectively training palliative care professionals has direct benefits to the critically ill patients and reduces the end-of-life distress for these patients' families. Adaptations within the Accreditation Council of Graduate Medical Education (ACGME) uphold resident physicians' formal training in palliative medicine and end-of-life symptom management. Such changes are preparing a critical mass of physicians in the United States to competently address seriously ill and dying patients' medical, emotional, and spiritual needs. Healthcare policy options dovetail with palliative medical education steadily at multiple levels of medical training—namely, medical school curriculum mandates, requiring residency training programs to foster patient-centered communication skills and discussions about advanced directives, and instituting palliative medicine proficiency Continuing Medical Education (CME) requirements for all states' medical licensing boards. Healthcare reform proposals must also evolve to redefine the National Health Service Corps (NHSC) post-graduate training over the next five years and the Hospice Medicare Benefit altogether. Clinical research in end of life care and leveraging Internet-based didactic technologies increase physicians' access to excellence in the field of hospice and palliative medicine. Correcting our current paucity of formal training in palliative medicine in the United States is a realistic goal and restores patients' dignity at the end of life.

Chapter 6 – End-of-life care (EOLC) decision-making plays a prominent role in the field of Gynecologic Oncology. Gynecologic oncologists are unique among surgical oncologists because they often become their patient's primary provider and are responsible for the patient's surgical and medical management. As a result, a close bond forms between the physician and the patient. The gynecologic oncologist is oftentimes the provider responsible for initiating EOLC conversations and making EOLC decisions with terminally ill patients. EOLC planning allows the patient to easily transition from the active treatment of cancer to the management of the physical, spiritual, and emotional needs of the dying patient. Without clear and frank discussions regarding patient preferences for EOLC, the patient's voice may get lost. Previous research has examined the importance of communication regarding EOLC preferences and has begun to lay the groundwork for effective dialogue between physicians and gynecologic oncology patients on this delicate topic. The main objective of this review is to evaluate the factors that play a role in the integration of EOLC into clinical practice.

Chapter 7 – Hospice decreases the fear of dying alone, reduces the agony of death, and helps in maintaining dignity at the end of life. Hospice holds a special place in the care of dying patients. However, the tendency to avoid the topic of death as well as complex Medicare rules surround it still make hospice an enigma. Some of the ethical issues surrounding hospice are: *A.* Should the referral to hospice be a prescription to abandon all hope? *B.* Should a hospice patient have to forgo all acute care? *C.* Can a patient with ongoing life sustaining treatment be referred to hospice? *D.* Should a current DNR order be a requirement for enrollment in hospice? *E.* Is palliative sedation acceptable for a hospice patient? *F.* Is talking about death a must? *G.* Is hospice care available only in institutions? *H.* What is the role of artificial hydration and nutrition in a hospice patient? *I.* How does one assess the decision-making capacity of a hospice patient? In this chapter, the authors will clarify these ethical issues in hospice, proving that hospice is not only ethically sound, but a good care alternative in thwarting the pain of fast approaching death.

In: Hospice Care
Editors: J. Hanl and S. Koeck

ISBN: 978-1-62618-456-5

Chapter 1

PROVIDING HOSPICE CARE TO LESBIAN, GAY, BISEXUAL AND TRANSGENDER (LGBT) POPULATIONS

Finn C. G. Reygan[1*] and Paul D'Alton[2]

[1] University of KwaZulu-Natal, Research Office, Govan Mbeki Centre, Westville Campus, Durban, South Africa

[2] St.Vincent's University Hospital, Department of Psycho-oncology, St.Vincent's University Hosptital, Elm Park, Dublin, Ireland

ABSTRACT

There is a growing research focus internationally on the healthcare needs of lesbian, gay, bisexual and transgender (LGBT) populations including in hospices and in palliative and end-of-life (EOL) care. Nevertheless LGBT patients too often remain invisible to healthcare providers who generally receive little or no training on the healthcare needs of these populations. Training lacunae and lack of LGBT cultural competencies have been shown to detrimentally affect the quality of care provided to LGBT patients in varied healthcare settings, including in

---

[*] Research and Professional Experience: Dr. Finn CG Reygan is a Postdoctoral Fellow at the University of KwaZulu-Natal in Durban, South Africa. He holds a PhD in Psychology, an MSc in Equality Studies and focuses on LGBT-related research, teaching and consultancy work in Europe, the USA and South Africa. He has published in a number of peer reviewed journals, including *Psycho-oncology*, *Perspectives in Education* and the *Journal of LGBT Youth*, has completed a number of funded research projects and presents internationally.

palliative and EOL care. In contrast, a growing number of professional bodies in the health sciences internationally are developing guidelines for healthcare providers on providing optimally managed care to LGBT populations. These guidelines require that healthcare providers become aware of the specific clinical issues as well as the socio-cultural and legal issues involved in providing care to LGBT people. In contrast to the general dearth of training in the area, a number of models of good practice with LGBT populations have been developed internationally. In this chapter we focus on one example which is work we developed in Ireland which prepares multidisciplinary healthcare teams to provide culturally sensitive and optimal palliative and EOL care to LGBT populations. This training module was developed on the premise that cross-cultural clinical competencies are increasingly being understood to include the healthcare needs of LGBT populations. Therefore this chapter outlines recent, evidence based research on the clinical needs of LGBT populations receiving palliative and EOL care; contextualises the personal histories and current socio-cultural concerns of LGBT populations; presents examples of good international practice in providing optimal care to LGBT populations; and offers recommendations for the inclusion of sexual and gender diversity into training programmes in the health sciences, specifically in hospice programmes.

Keywords: LGBT, hospice, palliative, EOL, diversity, sexuality, gender

Introduction

There is a growing body of research transnationally on the lives of lesbian, gay, bisexual and transgender (LGBT) populations across the lifespan, including research on end-of-life (EOL) and palliative care needs of LGBT populations (see Almack, Seymour and Bellamy, 2010; Harding, Epiphaniou and Chidgey-Clark, 2012; Rawlings, 2012; Reygan and D'Alton, 2012). This increased focus on the health and well-being of LGBT populations is occurring in tandem with an increased focus on the human rights of LGBT people globally (see www.ilga.org), including the introduction of same-sex civil unions and marriage rights in a number of jurisdictions. Even in countries that have a more favourable legislative and cultural climate for LGBT people prejudice and discrimination persist, including among healthcare professionals (Heaphy and Yip, 2006). This macro picture of LGBT rights globally is relevant to the provision of optimal, culturally sensitive care, including hospice care, to LGBT populations. In this regards there are a number of specific issues in care provision to LGBT people that healthcare providers need to be aware of and which we will explore in greater detail in this chapter. For example, LGBT people are often, though not always, a 'hidden population' and may therefore be invisible to healthcare providers.

Discriminatory legislation and a hostile social and cultural environment often impact on the health and wellbeing of LGBT people and lead to particular psychological and physical healthcare needs arising from experiences of 'minority stress' (see Mayock, Bryan, Carr and Kitching, 2009).

Healthcare providers need to be cognizant of these and other issues when providing optimal and psychologically sensitive care to LGBT populations. This professional sensitivity and competence is particularly important given the historical and ongoing pathologisation and marginalization of LGBT people in many contexts, including barriers to accessing and receiving healthcare services in hospice care. For example, groundbreaking research by Kathryn Almack (2010) in the United Kingdom found that LGB patients face particular issues in palliative and EOL care, including but not limited to homophobia and the invisibility of same-sex relationships in these services.

As a result of these concerns, this chapter briefly surveys the general health needs of LGBT populations before focusing on specific LGBT palliative and EOL care needs. Given the absence of a strong evidence base regarding LGBT EOL care, it is necessary to rely on general LGBT health research so as to better understand the specific EOL needs of these populations.

In so doing we hope to provide the reader who has little or no training on working with LGBT patients with a general overview of the area as well as an introduction to issues related specifically to providing hospice care to LGBT people. In the absence of face-to-face training on these issues we also provide a practical, five step guide to working with LGBT patients that we hope will be useful for practitioners.

These straightforward guidelines, developed in Ireland, have become a model of good practice and clinicians across health care settings have reported on their helpfulness and applicability.

General LGBT Health

Health disparities between LGBT and heterosexual/non-transgender populations have been a focus of research since the 1970s and the national health care agendas of a number of countries now include a focus on LGBT health, including the British Department of Health's Sexual Orientation and Gender Identity Advisory Group and the US Center for Disease Control and Prevention (Clarke, Ellis, Peel and Riggs, 2010). The US National Gay and Lesbian Task Force defines gay and lesbian health issues as 'diseases or conditions which are unique, more prevalent, more serious and for which risk factors and interventions are different' compared with heterosexuals (Plumb, 1997: 365). LGBT populations are not homogenous and vary in terms of race, class, gender and sexual orientation though the research has typically focused on the health of lesbian women and gay men and to a much lesser extent on bisexual and trans people's health. It is important to point out that the healthcare needs of LGBT people are often similar to the health needs of any other group of people. However, there are also specific LGBT healthcare needs which are often related to experiences of marginalization and discrimination. The LGBT health-related research has focused on a number of areas that are relevant for healthcare professionals providing hospice care to LGBT populations including, but not limited to, substance use, cancer care and mental health concerns.

A number of studies have found higher rates of substance use among LGBT populations compared with heterosexual/non-trans populations, including alcohol (see Hughes and Eliason, 2002; Lee, 2000), cigarettes (Ryan et al., 2001) and illicit drugs (Hyde et al., 2007). Clarke et al. (2010: 142) highlight a number of possible reasons for the higher levels of substance use among LGBT populations compared with heterosexual/non-trans populations, including the focus on bars and clubs in urban areas among LGBT social networks as well as substance use as a 'survival strategy' in the face of homophobia. Whatever the reasons for this higher prevalence, these health related behaviours contribute to chronic illness in later life among LGBT populations. In terms of mental health, studies indicate that LGBT people are at greater risk of mental illness compared with heterosexual/non-trans populations. This includes higher rates of depression and anxiety (see Koh and Ross, 2006; Pitts et al., 2006; Pitts et al., 2009) as well as higher rates of suicidal ideation, particularly among LGBT young people (see Roberts et al., 2004; Warner et al., 2004). Transgender people face mental health challenges (McNeil, Bailey, Ellis, Morton and Regan, 2012), as do bisexual people (Page, 2004), and this includes negative experiences with healthcare providers.

With reference to oncology, O'Hanlan (2006) points out that lesbian women have more risk factors for a number of cancers including fewer pregnancies, alcohol use, tobacco use and obesity. Valanis, Bowen, Bassford,

Whitlock, Charney and Carter (2000) indicate that lesbian women may attend for fewer mammograms and have higher rates of breast cancer. They also point out that reduced rates of pregnancy and less use of contraceptives, along with risk of overweight and endometriosis, may lead to an increase in ovarian and uterine carcinomas among lesbian women. Dibble, Roberts and Nussey (2004) found that, compared with heterosexual women, lesbian women had a significantly higher 5-year and lifetime risk for developing breast cancer. In relation to men who have sex with men (MSM), Goldstone et al. (2011) state that a number of studies point towards a higher prevalence of human papilloma virus (HPV) among MSM and suggest that these higher prevalence rates may be associated with higher incidence of anal cancer. In this regards, Chin-Hong et al. (2005) found that MSM who were sexually active had a high prevalence of anal squamous intraepithelial lesions (ASILs) which may result from continuing exposure to HPV.

In short, LGBT populations face a number of specific health-related challenges, which are often related to ongoing experiences of marginalisation and discrimination and resulting health-related behaviours. We highlight below some, but not all, of the factors that contribute to ill health among LGBT populations, all of which are relevant to healthcare provision in hospice and palliative care settings. The challenges that LGBT people face in terms of EOL and palliative care include: minority stress; lack of healthcare provider training; cohort differences; religious homophobia; and LGBT invisibility and disenfranchised grief.

LGBT Minority Stress

Psychological models of stress often include physical, emotional and cognitive components and present symptoms that clinicians can recognise. In this sense, while small amounts of stress may be beneficial and motivating, excessive stress leads to a number of problems including: anxiety; depression; social withdrawal; a sense of being overwhelmed; reduced appetite; panic attacks; insomnia; heart problems; and sexual dysfunction. The presence of these symptoms as a result of acute or chronic stress may lead to disease. Recent research on LGBT health has focused on ‘minority stress’ or rather on the stress that results from the chronic exposure of minority populations to ongoing discrimination. The minority stress model is a conceptual framework for exploring the negative impact on health and well-being of stigmatising social contexts (Brooks, 1981; Meyer, 1995, 2003). It includes the negative effects of stigmatization, social exclusion, discrimination and harassment on the mental health of minority groups such as LGBT people and which puts these groups at higher risk for mental health problems (Mayock et al., 2009). The literature indicates that, while social and structural factors lead to elevated mental health risks among LGBT people, greater equality and inclusion of LGBT people reduces this symptomology:

> The research…shows that being LGBT per se is not indicative of or correlated with mental health problems, and finds that the greater the support, inclusion and equality for LGBT people, the lesser the minority stress. (Mayock et al., 2009: 14)

Mayock et al. (2009: 14) found that the psychological distress of LGBT people was strongly correlated with external stressors including presumed heterosexuality, prejudice, victimization and homophobia. Internal stressors were associated with the anxiety of coming out, the negative reactions of others as well as the stress of self-concealment in contexts such as schools and workplaces. Clarke et al. (2010: 135) suggest that widespread social stigma puts LGBT people at greater risk of mental distress and Greene (1997) has pointed to the risk of 'double jeopardy' among LGBT racial and cultural minorities who are marginalized within their racial and cultural communities for being LGBT and excluded from LGBT communities as a consequence of white ethnocentricity. The health-related consequences of minority stress are also exacerbated by the lack of training on LGBT populations and their needs among healthcare providers and this has implications in terms of hospice care.

Lack of Training

Existing literature highlights the general lack of training on the needs of LGBT populations among healthcare providers, including among EOL and palliative care providers. The research also points to the prevalence of heterosexism and homophobia in health services, as reported by LGB[1] patients and in providers' attitudes towards LGB patients (see Beehler, 2001; Eliason and Schope, 2001; Hinchcliff et al., 2005). Peterson (1996) suggests that these disparities result from societal and interpersonal prejudice against LGBT

[1] While this chapter engages with the health of LGBT people some studies engage with specific cohorts within these populations, such as lesbian, gay and bisexual (LGB) or only transgender (T) people. Where this is the case the appropriate acronym is used.

people in health care services and among health care professionals. The Irish College of General Practitioners (ICGP) (Allen, 2008) points out that LGB patients may receive sub-optimal care as a result of anti-gay bias on the part of healthcare providers. In this regards, LGBT populations in Ireland continue to face many of the same challenges as LGBT people elsewhere when it comes to accessing health services. For example, Mayock et al. (2009) found that healthcare providers knew about their patients' LGBT identities less than 50% of the time, that LGBT patients were reluctant to disclose their identities and related health concerns due to fear of a negative response, and only 40% of LGBT people felt respected by their healthcare provider. In response to this healthcare exclusion, the ICGP points out that inclusive practice necessitates both familiarity with the specific health issues of patients who are LGB and the delivery of appropriate and accessible health services to these populations. As a result the ICGP advocates that General Practitioners be provided with the right resources to deliver competent care to LGB patients. The Irish Institute of Mental Health Nursing (IIMHN) (Higgins and Allen, 2010), also points out that mental health nurses need to be aware of the specific health needs and concerns of LGB patients, and states that anti-gay bias falls below the professional standards of the IIMHN. Therefore the IIMHN argues that the provision of inclusive mental health services must include a sufficient understanding of LGB issues including: minority stress; suicidal behaviour; grief; LGB parenting; self-harm; depression; and resilience. While some of these issues may be specific to LGBT populations, such as minority stress and LGBT parenting, others are more general health concerns. Nevertheless they can also be specific risk factors for LGBT people that mental health services could be aware of. In short, while there appears to be a general lack of training on LGBT populations among healthcare providers, professional bodies in a number of jurisdictions are beginning to develop good practice guidelines in this regards which have direct relevance for hospice care provision. As previously highlighted, LGBT populations are not homogenous and vary according to age, among others, and these differences require specific cultural competencies and sensitivity on the part of healthcare providers.

Cohort Differences

While EOL and palliative care are not the exclusive domain of older people, hospice care services present particular challenges for older LGBT people. As Blando (2001: 87) highlights, older LGBT people are an additionally hidden cohort within an often hidden population, the most invisible members within a minority that is often itself invisible. Given the generally heterosexist approach of much gerontological research, much remains to be known about older LGBT people. Nevertheless the international literature has begun to explore the experiences of this older LGBT cohort. It appears that ageism in LGBT communities as well as heterosexism among EOL and palliative care services further marginalizes and invisibilises older LGBT people. Also, as is often the case in much of the literature, bisexual and trans people receive much less research attention than gay men and lesbian women. For example, Age Concern England (ACE: now Age UK) (2007), notes that while older trans people share some issues in common with LGB people, they also face a unique set of challenges and are beginning to be seen as a recently emerging population with their own needs (Witten, 2002, 2003; Witten and Whittle, 2004). There is also a growing body of research on older bisexual people's health (Jones, 2012). One of the concerns of both older and younger LGBT cohorts is the influence of religion and religious ethos on the provision of healthcare, including in palliative and EOL care.

Religious Homophobia

Spirituality and religion may provide important succour to people receiving EOL and palliative care. However LGBT people may have a challenging, negative relationship with religion given the pervasiveness of religious homophobia. LGBT people follow multiple avenues in their atheist, spiritual and religious lives (Lease, Horne, Noffsinger-Frazier, 2005). In particular Yip (2005) outlines the numerous approaches LGB individuals employ when responding to religious exclusion and Yip (1997) found that concerns over stigmatization in religious communities means that some obscure their sexual orientation or abandon religion altogether. The literature indicates that religious homophobia is prevalent and Lease et al. (2005) point to the general assumption that LGBT people will be areligious because religious homophobia is prevalent. Yip (2000) found that some LGB people maintain their own private faith through prayer away from religious communities. Other researchers such as Lukenbill (1998) and Rodriguez and Ouellette (2000) found that some LGB people search out more welcoming religious communities. Mahaffy (1996) and Rodriguez and Ouellette (2000a) also point to the cognitive stress among LGB people who attempt to embody both a religious and LGB identity in non-affirming religious communities.

Schuck and Liddle (2001) found that LGB people may experience internal conflict, depression, shame, self-rejection and suicidal ideation resulting from the conflict between their religious and LGB identities. A number of researchers have also found a pernicious effect of organized religion on the health and wellbeing of LGB people (see Gage Davidson, 2000; Mahaffy, 1996; Rodriguez and Ouellette, 2000a; and Ritter and Terndrup, 2002). This may be the consequence of anti-gay religious teachings, the rejection of openly gay ministers and as a result of the isolation of LGB people in religious communities. Lease et al. (2005) suggest that most denominations struggle with the idea of homosexuality and that constant exposure to negative religious teaching among LGBT people may lead to negative perceptions of homosexuality on an individual and more general level. We argue that being cared for in a hospital or hospice setting that is religious may lead to the re-emerging or re-awakening among LGBT people of early negative experiences of religious homophobia. This is something that healthcare providers may not be aware of and therefore unprepared to address.

LGBT Invisibility and Disenfranchised Grief

The lack of same-sex civil unions and same-sex marriage legislation in many jurisdictions presents significant challenges for LGBT people receiving EOL and palliative care, their partners, friends and families. This is because the loss of a same-sex partner may be invisible to the larger world, especially among older LGBT cohorts who were forced to live much of their lives in secrecy given prevailing homophobia (Clarke et al., 2008). Researchers such as Shernoff (1998) and Whipple (2006) have found that same-sex partners may be removed from the decision making process regarding life support, funeral plans and life-saving interventions for their dying or deceased life partner. They may also face court action to remain in the family home and to access the couple's shared financial resources. Overall invisibility is one of the major challenges for LGBT people in society at large and when accessing health services, including EOL and palliative care. Having lived much of their lives in hostile social and legislative contexts, older LGBT people in particular and LGBT people living or working in homophobic environments remain 'in the closet' so as to avoid bias, discrimination and violence.

A study of same-sex bereavement in Ireland by Higgins and Glacken (2009) points to mixed experiences of LGB palliative and EOL care. In that study one participant recounted his experience of invisibility and consequent disenfranchised grief:

> I remember people saying to me "You've lost a good friend" and I felt something almost clicking in my head and thinking, I almost exploded, because I thought "I haven't lost a friend, I've lost someone that's been part of my life for 25 years, since I was 18....And I thought—a friend, I haven't lost a friend. Yes, I've lost a friend, but I have lost SO much more, and I actually remember thinking, 'You've no idea'".

Following Doka (1989), the various aspects of disenfranchised grief are all relevant for LGBT people, and particularly older LGBT people. In this regards Clarke et al. (2008: 232) point out that LGBT relationships may not be recognized because the couple were not 'out' or others refused to recognize the existence of the couple. LGBT loss may also not be acknowledged as a genuine loss because the relationship is not seen as being on an equal footing with an opposite sex relationship. The grievers may also remain unrecognized because friends often function as family for LGBT people, given hostility and ambivalence on the part of families-of-origin. However these families/ friendship networks may not be understood by healthcare providers. Finally, the death may not be socially sanctioned, such as by suicide or AIDS-related illness, and therefore does not receive the same supports. Nevertheless, despite experiences of marginalisation and discrimination and subsequent experiences of minority stress and negative health-related behaviours, LGBT populations also show resilience in the face of these life challenges and losses. This resilience and the strength that comes with it are also relevant in terms of hospice care to these populations.

LGBT Resilience

LGBT people display high levels of resilience in the face of, at times severe, challenges (Fredriksen-Goldsen, Kim, Emlet, Muraco, Erosheva, Hoy-Ellis, Goldsen and Petry, 2011). In this sense attachment theory (Bowlby, 1978a, b), probably one of the most influential theories in modern psychology, asserts that early life experiences with primary caregivers strongly influences the formation of internal models of relationships, and is to some extent understood as forming a template for how we function in relationships throughout life. The idea that affectional bonds provide us with safety and well-being and the thought or realization that they will be severed through death is, in simple terms, stressful. Obstacles to the development of these ties and their subsequent severing through homophobia, marginalization and ostracisation may impact negatively on the health and well-being of LGBT people. Erickson's (1950) developmental theory also elaborated on relationships of trust and mistrust and some of the later stages in this developmental arc may be challenging for LGBT people due to the homophobia present in families, schools, workplaces, healthcare settings and society at large.

Our sense of self is also in many ways contingent on interpersonal attachments (Baumeister and Lacy, 1995) but there are challenges for many LGBT people forming relationships because of internalized homophobia and lack of trust due to chronic experiences of marginalisation and discrimination. In short, there may be additional challenges for LGBT people in forming relationships and then in separating from them. Nevertheless, LGBT populations have responded to these challenges in numerous ways such as with: community organisations; the formation of de facto families with other LGBT people; political activism to bring about social change; and the development of psychological resilience. These are all behaviours that help LGBT populations to speak out and demand respectful and sensitive care from healthcare providers, as well as having their life experiences and relationship ties recognised in healthcare settings, even in the absence of appropriate legislation, policy and healthcare provider training on the needs of LGBT populations.

Hospice Care with LGBT Patients: The Guide

In Ireland the Hospice Friendly Hospitals (2010: 95) 'Quality Standards for End-of-Life Care in Hospitals' report defines palliative care to include a 'whole person approach which takes into consideration a person's circumstances, spirituality and sexuality'. In this way palliative care is holistic and considers the individual's sexuality. However the lack of research on LGBT palliative and EOL care exists despite, as highlighted above, the specific EOL needs of LGBT people. In the US, the Institute of Medicine (2011) has highlighted the lack of LGBT EOL and palliative care research and in the UK the 'EOLC Strategy Equality Impact Assessment' also noted a lack of evidence but suggests that sexual orientation and gender identity are the most likely areas for inequality and discrimination to occur in EOL care (DoH, 2008). In the UK the NHS National End of Life Care Programme also has a focus on achieving quality EOL care for LGBT people (see: www.endoflifecareforadults.nhs.uk/publications/rts-lgbt). In this broad context a model has emerged from Ireland in recent years on delivering optimal, psychologically sensitive, EOL and palliative care to LGBT patients (Reygan and D'Alton, 2012).

As is often the case globally, the development of services to LGBT populations in Ireland occurred in tandem with legislative and policy advances in the area. There have been significant changes in the realities of LGBT life in Ireland in recent decades such as the decriminalization of male homosexuality in 1993, the introduction of the Civil Partnership Act in 2011 and the passing of comprehensive equality legislation. The professional bodies have noted both LGBT health disparities and LGBT people's negative experiences of healthcare provision and have formulated professional guidelines for their members. The ICGP (Allen, 2008) and the IIMHN (Higgins and Allen, 2010) in conjunction with the Gay and Lesbian Equality Network (GLEN) have presented five step guidelines to good practice with LGB patients. These five step guidelines are relevant for a broad spectrum of health and social care professionals, including nursing and medical staff, social workers and psychologists among others, and in the provision of hospice care to LGBT patients.

Guidelines for healthcare staff working with lesbian, gay and bisexual patients:

1. Stay informed on LGB health issues
2. Don't assume all patients are heterosexual
3. Respond positively when patients disclose they are LGB
4. Challenge anti-gay bias and take a gay affirmative approach
5. Demonstrate that your practice is inclusive of LGB people (for example, put up an inclusive poster in your waiting room)

Reygan and D'Alton (2012) used these guidelines to develop their training programme for multidisciplinary oncology and palliative care staff in acute hospital and hospice settings. The training programme aimed to support these staff in delivering affirmative care to their LGBT patients, families and partners. The programme also aimed to increase staff awareness of help-seeking behaviours in these settings among LGBT patients. Importantly, the training programme provided participants with training materials that were considered to be easily accessible and that could be transferred to other oncology and palliative care services. During the training Reygan and D'Alton (2012) provided participants with recent research on the health needs, including the palliative and EOL care needs, of LGBT populations. A core aspect of the training was to open a space in the training workshops for healthcare providers to think, often for the first time, about the experience of LGBT patients in their services. In this sense, participants became sensitised to the relevant issues and began to move away from the assumption that all patients would be heterosexual or normatively gendered. Participants were guided through appropriate, supportive and professional responses to a patient disclosing their LGBT identity. Participants were also encouraged to create an inclusive and non-discriminatory environment in their healthcare facility and to clearly demonstrate to colleagues, patients and visitors that their healthcare facility was an inclusive and welcoming space.

Given the changed cultural climate in Ireland, the guidelines from the professional bodies outlined above and the inclusion of sexual orientation in the Health Service Executive's 'Patient Charter', there has been a gradual mainstreaming of LGBT needs in healthcare provision in Ireland. As a result Reygan and D'Alton (2012) found that their LGBT training was well received by stakeholders, participants and the organisations in which it was rolled out. Because of the success of the training Reygan and D'Alton (2012) recommended that it be rolled out nationwide in healthcare settings; that it be introduced on undergraduate and postgraduate courses for trainee healthcare providers; and that it be part of online educational initiatives and training for the continuing professional development of healthcare providers. In short, this training programme points to the applicability, usefulness and need for training on LGBT health for healthcare providers working with LGBT patients, including in palliative and hospice settings.

CONCLUSION

The human rights of LGBT people are beginning to be recognised on a global level and the United Nations recently included gay rights under the rubric of human rights for the first time. However LGBT populations still face significant challenges globally both in terms of their human rights and in terms of their physical and mental health and well-being. Nevertheless, given the emerging research on the palliative and EOL care experiences of LGBT populations, we are beginning to understand the challenges that these populations face when accessing and receiving optimal, culturally and psychologically senstive care. Given the gap in training of many healthcare professionals when it comes to the needs of sexual and gender minority populations, a growing number of interventions are being developed to fill this need. A project to train multidisciplinary, oncology and palliative care providers in hospitals and hospices in Dublin used a simple five step model in providing sensitive and evidence-based care to LGBT populations. This initiative is not an isolated one and reflects the growing awareness among hospice and palliative care organisations of the importance of LGBT cultural sensitivity and the need for professional competencies in this area, especially given the increasing visiblility of LGBT populations globally.

APPENDIX A

LGBT-related terminology (adapted from Mayock et al., 2009)

Bisexual: term used to describe anyone sexually and romantically attracted to both males and females.

Gay: a man whose primary sexual and romantic attraction is to other men. The term is more commonly applied to men who self-identify as same sex attracted, rather than men who have sex with men (MSM) but do not self-identify as gay.

While many women identify as gay, the term lesbian is commonly used to describe same-sex attracted women.

Lesbian: a woman whose primary sexual and romantic attraction is to other women. This term often refers to women who are same sex attracted rather than women who have sex with other women (WSW) but do not self-identify as lesbian.

LGB: acronym for lesbian, gay and bisexual. Sometimes written as GLB.

LGBT: acronym for lesbian, gay, bisexual and transgender. Sometimes written as GLBT.

Heteronormativity: the assumption that heterosexuality and heterosexual norms are universal, or at least the only acceptable conditions.

Closely related to heterosexism (see below), heteronormativity negatively affects LGBT people in a variety of ways, from actively oppressing those who do not fulfil heterosexual expectations to rendering them invisible.

Heterosexism: the presumption that heterosexuality is the norm or standard or is considered the 'natural' or superior sexual preference.
Heterosexual: a person whose primary sexual and romantic attraction is to people of the opposite sex. The term 'straight' is also sometimes used.
Homophobia: describes a fear, dislike or hatred of same-sex relationships, of gays and lesbians, and/or of one's own feelings for individuals of the same gender.
'Out', 'Coming out' is the more or less public act of declaring oneself lesbian, gay, bisexual or transgender. A person may be out in selected circumstances such as to friends, but not to family, co-workers or neighbours.
'Coming out' may also be used to describe the process through which transgender people come to recognise and publicly acknowledge their gender identity.
Transgender: an umbrella term to refer to people whose gender identity and/or gender expression differ(s) from the sex assigned to them at birth.

REFERENCES

Age Concern England (ACE) (2007) *Planning for later life: transgender people [information sheet]*. London: Age Concern England.

Allen, O. (2008). Lesbian, gay and bisexual patients: The issues for general practice. Available from: http://www.glen.ie/press/pdfs/LesbianGayandBisexualPatients-TheIssuesforGeneralPractice.pdf. Last accessed: 29th September 2010.

Almack, K. (2010) Exploring the impact of sexual orientation on experiences and concerns about end of life care and on bereavement for lesbian, gay and bisexual older people. *Sociology*, 44(5): 908-924.

Beehler, G.P. (2001) Confronting the culture of medicine: gay men's experiences with primary health care physicians. *Journal of the Gay and Lesbian Medical Association*, 5(4), 135-41.

Bowlby, J. (1978a) Attachment. In: *Attachment and Loss* (vol. 1) (2nd ed.). Harmondsworth: Penguin.

Bowlby, J. (1978b). Separation: anxiety and anger. In: *Attachment and Loss* (vol. 2). Harmondsworth: Penguin.

Blando, J.A. (2001) Twice hidden: older gay and lesbian couples, friends, and intimacy. *Generations*, 25(2), 87-89.

Brooks, V.R. (1981) *Minority Stress and Lesbian Women*. Lexington, MA: Lexington Books.

Case, P., Austin, S.B., Hunter, D.J., Manson, J.E., Malspeis, S. and Willett, W.C. (2004) Sexual orientation, health risk factors, and physical functioning in the Nurses' Health Study II. *Journal of Women's Health*, 13, 1033-47.

Chin-Hong, P.V., Vittinghoff, E., Cranston, R.D. et al. (2005) Age-related prevalence of anal cancer precursors in homosexual men: the EXPLORE study. *Journal of the National Cancer Institute*, 97(12), 896-905.

Clarke, V., Ellis, S., Peel, E. and Riggs, D. (2010) *Lesbian, gay, bisexual, trans and queer psychology: An introduction*. Cambridge: Cambridge University Press.

Cochran, S.D., Mays, V.M., Bowen, D. et al. (2001) Cancer related risk indicators and preventive screening behaviours among lesbians and bisexual women. *American Journal of Public Health*, 91, 591-597.

Dibble, S.L., Roberts, S.A. and Nussey, B. (2004) Comparing breast cancer risk between lesbians and their heterosexual sisters. *Women's Health Issues*, 14, 60-68.

Dillon, M. (1999). *Catholic identity*. Cambridge: Cambridge University Press.

Eliason, M.J. and Schope, R. (2001) Does 'don't ask don't tell' apply to health care? Lesbian, gay and bisexual people's disclosure to health care providers. *Journal of the Gay and Lesbian Medical Association*, 5(4), 125-34.

Erikson, E. (1973) Childhood and society. Harmondsworth: Penguin.

Fredriksen-Goldsen, K. I., Kim, H.-J., Emlet, C. A., Muraco, A., Erosheva, E. A., Hoy-Ellis, C. P., Goldsen, J. and Petry, H. (2011) *The aging and health report: disparities and resilience among lesbian, gay, bisexual, and transgender older adults-Key findings fact sheet.* Seattle: Institute for Multigenerational Health.

Frisch, M., Smith, E., Grulich, A. and Johansen, C. (2003) Cancer in a population-based cohort of men and women in registered homosexual partnerships. *American Journal of Epidemiology*, 157, 966-72.

Frisch, M., Biggar, R.J. and Goedert, J.J. (2000) Human papillomavirus-associated cancers in patients with human immunodeficiency virus infection and acquired immunodeficiency syndrome. *Journal of the National Cancer Institute*, 92, 1500-10.

Gage Davidson, M. (2000). Religion and spirituality. In R. M. Perez, K. A. DeBord and K. J.

Bieschke (eds.), *Handbook of counseling and psychotherapy with lesbian, gay and bisexual clients* (pp.409-433). Washington, DC: American Psychological Association.

Goldstone, S., Palefsky, J.M., Giuliano, A.R., Moreira, J., Aranda, C. et al. (2011) Prevalence of and risk factors for human papillomavirus (HPV) infection among HIV-seronegative men who have sex with men. *Journal of Infectious Diseases*, 203, 66-74.

Greene, B. (1997) Ethnic minority lesbians and gay men: mental health and treatment issues. In B. Greene (ed.), *Ethnic and cultural diversity among lesbians and gay men* (pp.216-39). London: Sage.

Harding, R., Epiphaniou, E. and Chidgey-Clark, J. (2012) Needs, experiences, and preferences of sexual minorities for end-of-life and palliative care: A systematic review. *Journal of Palliative Medicine*, 15(5), 602-611.

Heaphy, B. and Yip, A.K.T. (2006) Policy implications of ageing sexualities. *Social Policy and Society*, 5(4), 443-451.

Higgins, A. and Allen, O. (2010) *Gay, lesbian and bisexual people: A good practice guide for mental health nurses*. Dublin: Irish Institute of Mental Health Nursing and GLEN.

Higgins, A., and Glacken, M. (2009) Sculpting the distress: easing or exacerbating the grief experience of same-sex couples. *International Journal of Palliative* Nursing, 15(4), 170-176.

Hinchcliff, S., Gott, M. and Galena, E. (2005) ‘I daresay I might find it embarrassing’: general practitioners’ perspectives on discussing sexual health issues with lesbian and gay patients. *Health and Social Care in the Community*, 13(4), 345-53.

Hospice Friendly Hospitals (2010) *Quality standards for end-of-life care in hospitals*. Dublin: Irish Hospice Foundation.

Hughes, T.L. and Eliason, M.J. (2002) Substance use and abuse in lesbian, gay, bisexual and transgender populations. *Journal of Primary Prevention*, 22(3), 263-298.

Institute of Medicine (2011) *The health of lesbian, gay, bisexual and transgender people. Building a foundation for better understanding*. Washington DC: National Academies Press.

Jones, R.L. (2012) Imagining the unimaginable: bisexual roadmaps for ageing. In R. Ward, I. Rivers and M. Sutherland (eds.), *Lesbian, gay, bisexual and transgender ageing: biographical approaches for inclusive care and support* (pp. 21–38). London: Jessica Kingsley.

Kelleher, C. (2009) Minority stress and health: Implications for lesbian, gay, bisexual, transgender, and questioning (LGBTQ) young people. *Counselling Psychology Quarterly*, 22(4), 373-379.

Kimmel, D.C., Rose, T. and David, S. (eds.) (2006) *Lesbian, gay, bisexual, and transgender aging: research and clinical perspectives*. New York: Columbia University Press.

Koh, A.S. and Ross, L.K. (2006) Mental health issues: a comparison of lesbian, bisexual, and heterosexual women. *Journal of Homosexuality*, 51(1), 33-57.

Lease, S., Horne, S. and Noffsinger-Frazier, N. (2005). Affirming faith experiences and psychological health for Caucasian lesbian, gay, and bisexual individuals. *Journal of Counselling Psychology*, 52(3), 378-388.

Lee, R. (2000) Health care problems of lesbian, gay, bisexual, and transgender patients. *Western Journal of Medicine*, 172, 403-408.

Leming, M.R. and Dickenson, G.E. (2002) *Understanding dying, death and bereavement*. Fort Worth, TX: Harcourt.

Lukenbill, B. (1998). Observations of the corporate culture of a gay and lesbian congregation. *Journal for the Scientific Study of Religion,* 37(3), 440-552.

Mahaffy, K. A. (1996). Cognitive dissonance and its resolution: A study of lesbian Christians. *Journal for the Scientific Study of Religion,* 35, 392-402.

Mayock, P., Bryan, A., Carr, N. and Kitching, K. (2009). *Supporting LGBT lives: A study of the mental health and well-being of gay, lesbian, bisexual and transgender people.* Dublin: Gay and Lesbian Equality Network (GLEN) and BeLonG To Youth Service.

McNeil, J., Bailey, L., Ellis, S., Morton, J. and Regan, M. (2012) Trans Mental Health Study 2012. Accessed on December 21st 2012 at: http://www.scottishtrans.org/Uploads/Resources/trans_mh_study.pdf

Meyer, I. (2003) Prejudice, social stress, and mental health in lesbian, gay and bisexual populations: Conceptual issues and research evidence. *Psychological Bulletin*, 129, 5, 674-697.

Meyer, I. (1995) Minority stress and mental health in gay men. *Journal of Health and Social Behavior*, 36, 38-56.

O'Hanlan, KA. (2006) Health policy considerations for our sexual minority patients. *Obstetrics and Gynecology*, 107(3), 709-714.

Page, E.H. (2004) Mental health services experiences of bisexual women and bisexual men: an empirical study. *Journal of Bisexuality*, 4(1-2), 137-160.

Peterson, K.J. (ed.) (1996) *Health care for lesbians and gay men: confronting homophobia and heterosexism*. Binghamton, NY: Harrington Park Press.

Pitts, M., Couch, M., Mulcare, H., Croy, S. and Mitchell, A. (2009) Health and wellbeing of trans people in Australia and New Zealand. *Feminism and Psychology*, 19(4), 475-495.

Pitts, M., Smith, A., Mitchell, A. and Patel, S. (2006) *Private lives: a report on the health and wellbeing of GLBTI Australians*. Melbourne: Australian Research Centre in Sex, Health and Society.

Plumb, M. (1997) Blueprint for the future: the lesbian health advocacy movement. In J. White and M. Martinez (eds.), *The lesbian health book: caring for ourselves* (pp.362-78). Seattle: Seal Press.

Rawlings, D. (2012) End-of-life care considerations for gay, lesbian, bisexual, and transgender individuals. *International Journal of Palliative Nursing*, 18(1), 29-34.

Ritter, K. Y. and Terndrup, A. I. (2002). *Handbook of affirmative psychotherapy with lesbians and gay men*. New York: Guilford Press.

Roberts, S.J., Grindel, C.G., Patsdaughter, C.A., Reardon, K. and Tarmina, M.S. (2004) Mental health problems and use of services of lesbians : results of the Boston lesbian health project II. *Journal of Gay and Lesbian Social Services : Issues in Practice, Policy and Research*, 17(4), 1-16.

Rodriguez, E. M. and Ouellette, S. C. (2000). Gay and lesbian Christians: Homosexual and religious identity integration in the members and participants of a gay-positive church. *Journal for the Scientific Study of Religion,* 39(3), 333-347.

Ryan, H., Wortley, P.M., Easton, A., Pederson, L. and Greenwood, G. (2001) Smoking among lesbians, gays, and bisexuals: a review of the literature. *American Journal of Preventive Medicine*, 21(2), 142-149.

Schuck, K. D. and Liddle, B. J. (2001). Religious conflicts experienced by lesbian, gay, and bisexual individuals. *Journal of Gay and Lesbian Psychotherapy,* 5(2), 63-82

Shernoff, M. (1998) *Gay widowers: life after the death of a partner*. New York: Harrington Park Press.

Shokeid, M. (1995). *A gay synagogue in New York*. New York, NY: Columbia University.

Stevens, P.E. (1992) Lesbian health care research: a review of the literature from 1970 to 1990. *Health Care for Women International*, 13(2), 91-120.

Valanis, B.G., Bowen, D.J., Bassford, T., Whitlock, E., Charney, P. and Carter, R.A. (2000) Sexual orientation and health: comparisons in the

Women's Health Initiative sample. *Archives of Family Medicine*, 9, 843-53.

Walter, C.A. (2003) *The loss of a life partner: narratives of the bereaved*. New York: Columbia University Press.

Warner, J., McKeown, E., Griffin, M., Johnson, K., Ramsay, A., Cort, C. and King, M. (2004) Rates and predictors of mental illness in gay men, lesbians and bisexual men and women. *British Journal of Psychiatry*, 185, 479-485.

Whipple, V. (2006) *Lesbian widows: invisible grief*. New York: Haworth Press.

Witten, T.M. (2002) Geriatric care and management issues for the transgendered and intersexed populations. *Geriatric Care and Management Journal*, 12(3), 20-24.

Witten, T.M. (2003) Transgender aging: an emerging population and an emerging need. *Sexologies*, 12, 14-19.

Witten, T.M. and Whittle, S. (2004) Transpanthers: the greying of transgender and the law. *Deakin Law Review*, 23, 1-17.

Yip, A. K. T. (1997). *Gay male Christian couples: Life stories*. Westport, CT: Praeger.

Yip, A. K. T. (2000). Leaving the church to keep my faith: The lived experiences of non-heterosexual Christians. In L. J. Francis and Y. J. Katz (eds.), *Joining and Leaving Religion* (pp.129-145). Leominster, UK: Gracewing.

Yip, A. K. T. (2003a). Spirituality and sexuality: An exploration of the religious beliefs of non-heterosexual Christians in Great Britain. *Theology and Sexuality*, 9(2), 137-54.

Yip, A. K. T. (2003b). The self as the basis of religious faith: Spirituality of gay, lesbian and bisexual Christians. In G. Davie, L. Woodhead and P. Heelas (eds.), *Predicting religion* (pp.135-146). Aldershot: Ashgate.

Yip, A. K. T. (2005). Queering religious texts: An exploration of British non-heterosexual.

Christians' and Muslims' strategy of constructing sexuality-affirming hermeneutics. *Sociology*, 39(1), 47-65.

RESOURCES

International Lesbian, Gay, Bisexual, Trans and Intersex Association (ILGA): www.ilga.org.

Irish Hospice Foundation booklet 'Coping with the death of a same-sex partner': www.hospicefoundation.ie/wp-content/uploads/2012/08/00298-14-IHF-Death-of-Same-Sex-Partner-V5.pdf.

Metropolitan Community Church (MCC): www.mcchurch.org.

National Coalition for LGBT Health: www.lgbthealth.net.

NHS End of Life LGBT Care Programme: wzww.endoflifecareforadults.nhs.uk/publications/rts-lgbt.

SAGE: Services and advocacy for gay, lesbian, bisexual and transgender elders webpage: www.sageusa.org.

The Fenway Institute and The National LGBT Health Education Center: www.lgbthealtheducation.org.

University of California at San Francisco, LGBT Centre: http://lgbt.ucsf.edu

US Center for Disease Control and Prevention (CDC). Lesbian, Gay, Bisexual and Transgender Health webpage: www.cdc.gov/lgbthealth.

In: Hospice Care
Editors: J. Hanl and S. Koeck

ISBN: 978-1-62618-456-5

Chapter 2

SOCIOLOGICAL EXPLANATIONS FOR THE QUALITY OF END-OF-LIFE CARE IN FINLAND

James M. Hoefler*
Department of Political Science, Dickinson College, Carlisle, PA, US

ABSTRACT

Tremendous strides have been made in the last two decades with regard to the quality of palliative care available to patients at the end of life. But progress has not been uniform across the countries of western and northern Europe. Despite its well-earned reputation as one of the generally progressive welfare states of greater Scandinavia, Finland (like its Nordic neighbours) tends to trail behind other western European countries when it comes to end-of-life care policies and practices. A comparative analysis of recent research on palliative care at the end of life, together with research on sociological perspectives related to the care of the dying in western Europe, suggests that cultural forces underlie the generally lower quality of end-of-life care in Scandinavia. At the same

* James M. Hoefler, Ph.D., is professor of political science at Dickinson College in Carlisle, PA, US. Professor Hoefler has written two books on end-of-life care in the United States and several articles and book chapters on end-of-life care in Europe. Professor Hoefler serves as the Coordinator for the Policy Studies program at Dickinson, serves as a board member of the of the Carlisle Area Health and Wellness Foundation, and serves on the biomedical ethics committee at the Carlisle Regional Medical Center.

time, there is evidence to suggest that Finland is generally well positioned to make advances in end-of-life care.

Keywords: Palliative care, terminal care, hospice, Finland, Denmark, Norway, Sweden, Scandinavia

INTRODUCTION

According to the World Health Organization (WHO), palliative care at the end of life – care concerned with the quality of life patients experience in their dying days – is one of the more important but neglected public health issues of our time. WHO identifies needs for improvements both in (1) training and education for care givers and (2) symptom management for patients (World Health Organization, 2009).

Advances in end-of-life care have been made in many countries in recent years. The UK has developed a solid reputation as a leader in end-of-life care, and other countries in central Western Europe (e.g., Ireland, Belgium, and Austria) have made important strides in this area as well. At the same time WHO notes that progress in adopting palliative care as a clinical priority has lagged elsewhere, even in many first-world countries. Data collected by the Economist Intelligence Unit on palliative care policies and practices across Western Europe suggest that Scandinavian countries (Finland, Denmark, Norway, Sweden) tend to register below (and often well below) the median on various dimensions of end-of-life care (see Figures 1 and 2 ; Economist Intelligence Unit, 2010).

The United Kingdom (GB) earned the highest *Quality of Death* score (1.8). The UK is especially strong in the areas of *quality* (blue bar) and *availability* (red bar) of end-of-life care, but falls down in the areas of *environment* (purple bar) and to a lesser degree, *cost* (green bar).

Norway and Sweden have overall *Quality of Death* scores just above the mean (0.3 and 0.2 respectively). Norway is relatively weak with regard to the *availability* of end-of-life care (red bar) and the end-of-life care *environment* (purple bar). Sweden is relatively weak in the areas of *quality* (blue bar) and *environment* (purple bar).

The Economist Intelligence Unit scored forty countries on four dimensions of end-of-life care, then weighted them to create an overall index they called "Quality of Death." The four dimensions and their index weighting are listed below:

***Quality* of End-of-Life Care (40%)**

- Public awareness of and government attitudes and policies related to end-of-life care (e.g., Do-Not-Resuscitate policies, availability of pain killers, etc.)
- Training and accreditation in the area of end-of-life
- Doctor-patient transparency

***Availability* of End-of-Life Care (25%)**

- Availability and use of hospice, palliative care services, and end-of-life care volunteer workers
- Existence of government-led palliative care strategy

End-of-Life Care *Environment* (20%)

- Political stability
- GDP per capita
- Old-age-dependency ratio
- Life expectancy
- Health care spending as a percentage of GDP
- Hospital beds, doctors, and nurses per capita
- Pension coverage
- Social security-related health care spending.

***Cost* of End-of-Life Care (15%)**

- Availability of public funding for end-of-life care
- Financial burden of end-of-life care to patients

Figure 1. Dimensions of end-of-life care.

Denmark's *Quality of Death* score falls below the normalized mean (-0.5) and Finland's falls substantially below the normalized mean (-1.3) for all countries in this western European subset. Denmark scores better than most countries in the subset when it comes to *cost* of end-of-life care (green bar), but is rated poorly on the other three dimensions of end-of-life care. Finland scores poorly across the board.

A review of the literature in the areas of palliative care resource allocation, medical training, clinical practice, and symptom management tends to corroborate the Economist Intelligence Unit's findings. This all begs the question: If Finland and its Nordic neighbours are typically known as progressive welfare states with relatively generous and equitably distributed social welfare benefits, why do these countries fare so comparatively poor when it comes to the *quality of death* each locale affords? And what is the prognosis for reversal of this trend? It is to these two fundamental questions that we now turn.

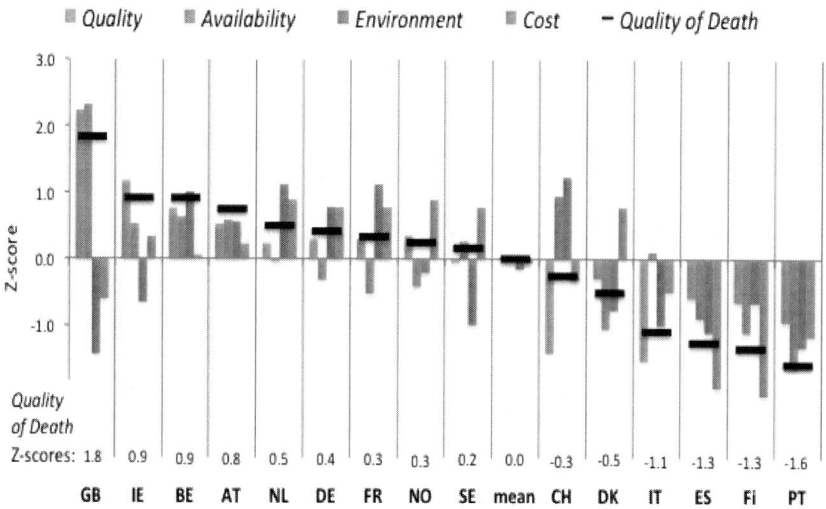

Figure 2. Z-scores for end-of-life care *Quality*, *Availability*, *Environment*, *Cost*, and *Quality of Death*.

METHODS

Data for this analysis were drawn from surveys of published research on sociological tendencies, cultural predispositions, and attitudinal surveys of patients, doctors, and the general public across Europe. Sources of this data included:

- The World Values Survey (WVS), the European Social Survey (ESS), and the Gallup World Survey, and;

- Recent medical literature and various associations of palliative care in Europe; data on pain and use of analgesia, quality of hospital care, and health care resource allocation across Europe.

All data sources reported comparative data that included Finland and at lease one other Scandinavian country whenever possible. All of the data collected for this report were drawn from sources published in the last ten years and the majority of the data is less than five years old.

RESULTS

The data reviewed below point to existence of a Scandinavian mindset – a state of mind which is (A) generally optimistic, (B) eschews exceptionalism, is characterised by (C) comparatively low levels of sympathy and (D) relatively high levels of regime support. This mindset may help explain why the otherwise progressive countries of northern Europe tend to fall short in the provision of palliative care.

A. Dispositional Optimism

The first Scandinavian norm suggested by the data is a tendency toward *dispositional optimism*: a generally positive and fatalistic expectancy that one will experience good outcomes (Wrosch & Scheier, 2003; Scheier & Carver, 1985; Hystad, Eid, Laberg, Johnsen, & Bartone, 2009). The residents of Scandinavian countries are annually reported to be among the happiest people in the world. The Gallup World Poll ranked Denmark, Finland, Norway, and Sweden (in that order) in the top four spots in its most recent survey of the world's happiest countries. Indeed, all four Scandinavian countries typically make the top-ten list of other researchers who have studied *happiness* and *satisfaction* in countries around the world (Helliwell, Layard, & Sachs, 2012; Inglehart, 2011). This is the case despite a northern European climate characterized much of the year by the kind of short, cool, snowy and rainy days that most consider less than optimal for engendering cheerfulness (see Figure 3).[1]

[1] Denmark, with the mildest climate of the four, has, on average, only 4 hours of sun per day and 170 days of rain a year, and a mean annual temperature of 47° F (8° C; BBC, 2010).

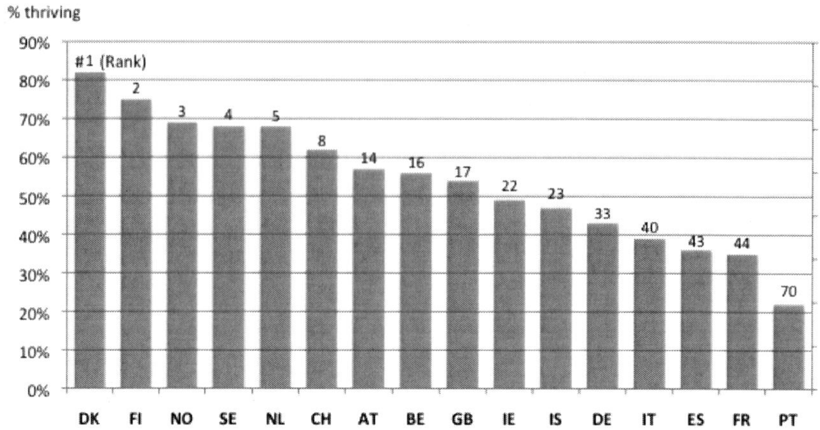

Figure 3. Percent of the population who report to be *thriving*.

Scandinavians specifically report being more satisfied with their health status than other Europeans, even though Scandinavians – Finns and Danes in particular – are likely to get sick and die sooner than residents of other countries in western Europe.[2] Death anxiety is prevalent in many cultures, and thinking about death often interferes with one's ability to be happy. Here again, however, Scandinavians (with the exception of Norwegians) distinguish themselves from the mainstream, as they are more likely than residents of most countries in western Europe to agree with the following statement: "Death is inevitable, it is pointless to worry about it" (Inglehart).

Medical treatment at the end of life is often futile and often only serves to exacerbate the patient's suffering. This is why patients in many first-world countries decide, in consultation with their physicians, to forgo some or all life-sustaining treatments as death approaches. This transition from care that is focused on sustaining life to care that emphasizes aggressive symptom management is not yet typical or routine, however. Rather, it requires that physicians and patients express some level of dissatisfaction with currently predominant western medical norms that focus on *cure* rather than *care*. Scandinavian countries rank low on measures associated with proactive management of the dying process and it could be argued that their

[2] Life expectancy is shorter only in Ireland and Portugal (University of California Atlas of Global Inequality, 2010).

dispositional optimism – the predisposition to be satisfied with *what is*, and not to agitate for what *might be* – is at least partly responsible.[3]

B. *Jante Law*

The *Jante Law* -- a term used to describe an informal pattern of group behaviour observed in Scandinavian countries -- is a second dimension of the Scandinavian mindset that may help explain its laggard status with regard to palliative care. [4] The Jante Law refers to the norms of behaviour detailed in Danish-Norwegian author Aksel Sandemose's fictional account of a small, narrow-minded Danish village called Jante (Sandemose, 1936; see Figure 4). Taken together, these norms emphasize the collective good and conformity to group norms while discouraging anything that has the potential to disrupt social stability. Exceptional achievement and the acquisition of specialized knowledge, especially when that knowledge is provided by outsiders, violate central tenants of the Jante Law.[5]

Do not:

- think you are anything special.
- think you are as important as we are.
- think you are wiser than we are.
- fool yourself into thinking you are better than we are.
- think you know more than we do.
- think you are more than we are.
- think that you are good at anything.
- laugh at us.
- think that anyone cares about you.
- think you can teach us anything.

Figure 4. The Jante Law's "Ten Commandments".

[3] There is also some evidence to suggest that high levels of dispositional optimism may lead to higher levels of psychophysical comfort in patients, and higher tolerance for pain. (Bargiel-Matusiewicz & Krzyszkowska, 2009; Geers, Wellman, Fowler, & Helfer, 2010).

[4] *Jante Law* is a common term in the native languages of all four Scandinavian countries addressed here. In Danish and Norwegian the term is *Janteloven*; in Swedish it is *Jantelagen*; in Finnish it is *Janten laki*.

[5] This tendency is sometimes referred to as *Tall Poppy Syndrome*, especially in Australia and New Zealand (Kirkwood, 2007).

The widely shared tendency to look disapprovingly on individual achievement and expertise, may help explain resistance to advances in palliative medicine where specialized knowledge is often required in order to provide first-rate end-of-life care. Policy makers in other countries have employed a number of approaches to improving the delivery of palliative care. Designation of faculty chairs in palliative care, establishing specialist credentials for health professionals in palliative care, borrowing heavily from treatment protocols developed in other countries, and requiring physicians to complete continuing medical education (CME) courses are four such approaches.

Scandinavian countries have lagged behind on credentialing palliative care programs and specialists and have been slow to adopt treatment protocols that have become standards of practice elsewhere in Europe. Perhaps most strikingly, the Scandinavian countries stand almost alone as the only countries remaining in western Europe where physicians are not required to acquire any advanced training once they have completed their basic medical education (see Figure 5; Desbois, Pardell, Negri, et al., 2010).

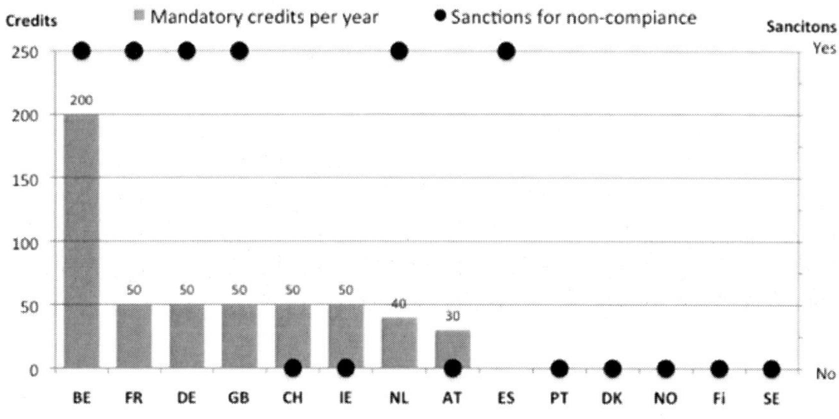

Figure 5. Continuing Medical Education Credit (CME) requirements.

Jante provides one explanation for this outcome: Designating specialist chairs, credentialing specialists in subfields, adopting clinical treatment protocols developed elsewhere, and requiring special CME training all run counter to the Jantian principles. As Dahl (p. 103) notes in his essay on the nature of Scandinavians: "Suspicion toward anything extraordinary is everywhere," and this appears to be one reason why all four Scandinavian countries have been slow to improve the care they provide to patients at the end of life (Dahl, 1984).

The low priority put on exceptional knowledge in Scandinavia may also be a reason why so few Scandinavian physicians have volunteered to serve on international working groups of palliative care experts. Finland and Denmark provide a good case in point. Switzerland, a country with only slightly more residents than either of these two countries, has seen nine of its medical experts serve on international palliative care boards since palliative medicine emerged in the early 1990s as an important cause among health care professionals. Finland and Denmark have each only contributed one such expert to the international effort. Germany is the only other country in Western Europe to contribute so little to international initiatives, but Germany has a robust internal effort to advance the cause of palliative care for end-of-life patients within its borders. Finnish and Danish efforts here are weak, at best. Only two of thirteen countries surveyed had weaker palliative care movements.

It would be a mistake to overstate the role Jante plays in modern-day, increasingly cosmopolitan Scandinavian countries. At the same time, it would be wrong to discount entirely the role Jantian predispositions continue to play in Nordic Europe. Culture changes slowly, even in an increasingly globalized world, and maybe even slower in these sparsely populated, culturally homogeneous lands where Jantian pride (sometimes masking as false humility) seems at work to inhibit advances in palliative care that are taking place elsewhere.[6]

C. The Empathy Gap

A third reason why Scandinavian countries may be lagging their Western European neighbours in the area of end-of-life care may have something to do with the *empathy gap*. Scandinavians report comparatively low levels empathy when it comes to assisting those most likely to need end-of-life care: those who are suffering and the elderly. Finland and Denmark, for example, rank at the bottom of the list of countries included in the World Values Survey regarding their "identification with suffering" and "moral duty to the elderly"

[6] Among the 15 western European countries ranked, Denmark trails only Finland, Austria, and Norway in its overall "self-image" (Reputation Institute, 2010).

as motivations for doing volunteer work with these groups (see Figure 6; Inglehart).

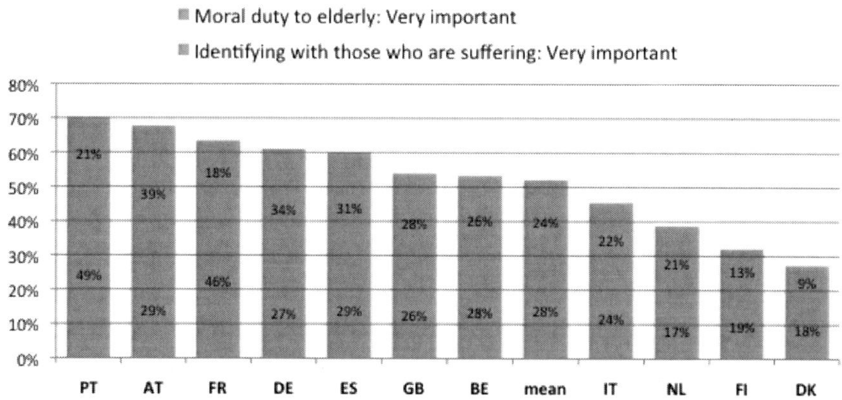

Figure 6. Motivations for doing volunteer work.

Comparative data on patient experiences with chronic pain – a common concern among end-of-life patients – suggests that Scandinavian physicians are also comparatively less than sympathetic toward patients in their care than elsewhere in Europe. In one recent study of chronic pain in Europe, Breivik, et al., reported that Danish and Norwegian doctors rated their patients' pain using the standard ten-point pain scale only six and five percent of the time, respectively. This placed these two countries twelfth and thirteenth among the fourteen Western European countries studied. A more recent study by Breivik (et al) suggests that Scandinavian doctors are generally more interested in treating a cancer patient's *cancer* than they are the cancer patient's *pain*. They are less likely to take the patients *quality of life* into account when making treatment decisions than doctors elsewhere in European. (Sweden is somewhat exceptional in this regard; see Figure 7; Breivik, Cherny, & Collett, 2009).

It may be presumptuous to conclude that Scandinavian doctors tend to have comparatively low levels of concern for patients who require palliative care services. For example, it may be that reluctance of doctors to ask patients about their pain or to take quality of life considerations into account can be attributed to a lack of training. It seems as likely as not, however, that lack of empathy is at least partly to blame given that Scandinavians, in general, report levels of empathy that are generally lower than elsewhere in Europe.

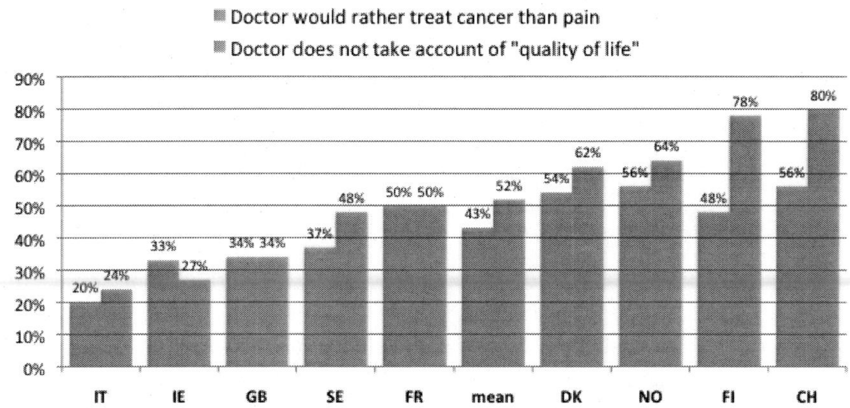

Figure 7. Patient reports of physician attitudes.

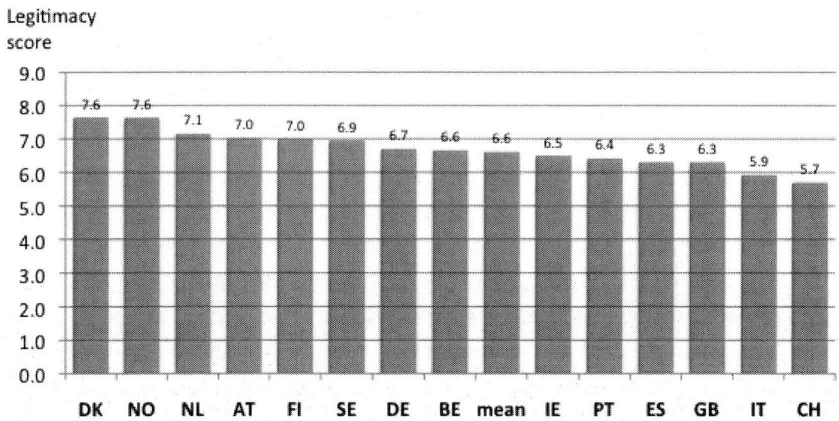

Figure 8. Political Legitimacy scores.

D. Political Legitimacy

Political legitimacy is the fourth dimension of the Scandinavian mindset that may help us understand the relatively weak state of palliative care in Nordic Europe. All countries have their internal critics and dissenters, and Scandinavian countries are no different in this regard. At the same time, residents of Scandinavian countries exhibit relatively high levels of confidence in their respective governments, in general, and in their respective health care systems in particular (Inglehart). As such, they may be less willing to question or complain about the resource allocation decisions that have very clearly short-changed attention to palliative care in their countries (see Figure 8; Gilley, 2006).

The general approach Scandinavians seem to take about their governments and their policies is this: *As long as all people are treated about the same, then no one has much reason to complain.* According to Norwegian journalist, historian and professor Hans F. Dahl, this *passion for equity*, which

> has been passed down from the nineteenth century and helped shape the political system of today is certainly a fine thing – so long as it does not prevent new ideas, new institutions, and novel interests to emerge in the fabric of Nordic society (Dahl).

On this point, it should be noted that the hospice movement is quite young in Scandinavia, and both professional and volunteer staff are still finding their way there. The development of hospice as a palliative care alternative for dying patients has strong roots in the not-for-profit sector where volunteer workers are still, in many respects, the lifeblood of the enterprise. It may be that hospice has taken a long time to take root in Scandinavia because people there are generally just less empathetic regarding the elderly and those who are suffering. It may also be true, however, that volunteer efforts in palliative care may be psychologically "squeezed out" by the welfare state, which is so well trusted and dominates so much of the social service sector in Scandinavia. That is, the natural impulse to contribute time and resources to charitable causes may have atrophied somewhat in Scandinavia where the breadth of the welfare state is so extensive that residents simply assume that if something should be done, the government will do it.

Evidence of this "squeezing out" effect is seen in the data on how family members prefer that care for an elderly parent be provided. Family members are typically called on to play a key role in providing end-of-life care, often in the parents' own home. But Figure 9 suggests that Scandinavians are much more likely to prefer that care of elderly relatives fall to nursing homes (dark red) and non-family care providers (light red), while they are less likely to favour being directly involved with the care either in their own homes (light green) or in the parents' home (dark green). It is easy to see that a robust hospice movement has had trouble taking root where such sentiments predominate. This kind of general "disengagement" with care of the elderly may also help explain why there generally seems to be less of a concern among Scandinavians regarding the quality of the end-of-life care provided in their countries (European Commission, 2007).

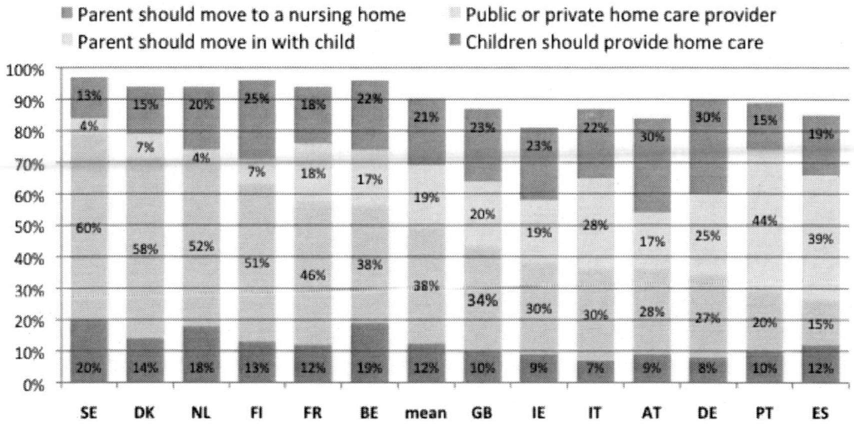

Figure 9. Caring for elderly parent preferences.

CONCLUSION

As a group, Danes, Norwegians, Swedes, and Finns share similarities in history, ethnicity, language (excepting the Finns), and culture that set them apart from the rest of Western Europe. These commonalities are well suited to development and persistence of the common Scandinavian mindset described above. Individually, these four Nordic countries are among the most ethnically homogenous nations in the Western world (Fearon, 2003). They each lack the kind of religious, ethnic, and cultural diversity that tends to erode common cultural predispositions in countries that have more diverse populations. In addition, these four countries are relatively small in population, and with the exception of Denmark, they are the most sparsely populated lands of Western Europe. Denmark, Norway, Sweden, and Finland have a combined population about half the population of Spain, sprinkled across a land mass twice as large. The ethnically homogeneous, sparsely populated countries of Scandinavia provide fertile ground for stable social norms that have roots deep enough to have a significant bearing on health policy, in general, and end-of-life care policy in particular.

At the same time, these four countries are not entirely similar. As already noted above, Swedish physicians seem to be better at managing pain than physicians elsewhere in Nordic Europe. And Sweden and Norway tend to score much better on *quality of death* indicators than Denmark and Finland.

Finland, too, shows evidence that they are not entirely like its Nordic neighbours, and several of these differences suggest that basic structures are in place in Finland that make gains in end-of-life care more likely than elsewhere in northern Europe. In fact, several recent studies, when taken together, suggest that Finland is well positioned to make gains in this area.

A. Quality of Care

One 2012 study on patient safety, satisfaction, and quality of hospital care indicates that Finnish patients rate the overall quality of their hospital care higher than patients in many other countries in Europe. Fully two-thirds of Finnish patients would recommend their hospital (compared to Spain where only 55% of patients would do so; see Figure 10; Aiken, Semeus, Van den Heede, et al., 2012).

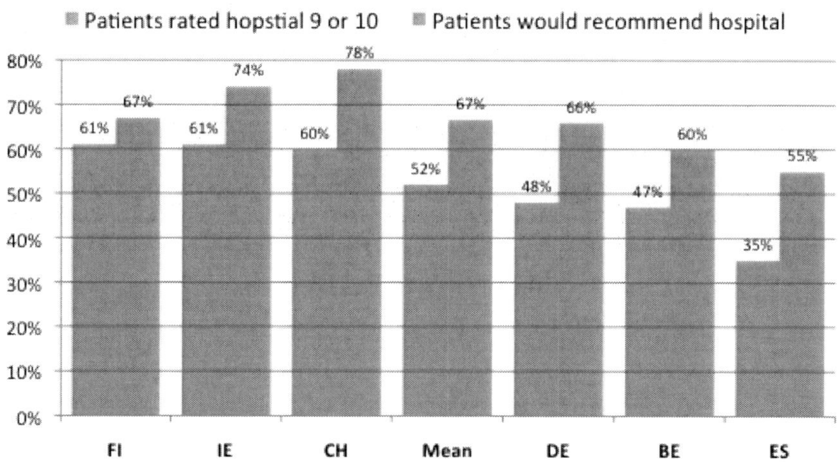

Figure 10. Patient satisfaction with hospital care.

Health care providers corroborate this general sense of quality in hospital care reported by Finnish patients. Only 13% of nurses in this same study reported their ward to have a poor quality of care, second only to Ireland in this regard (see Figure 11).

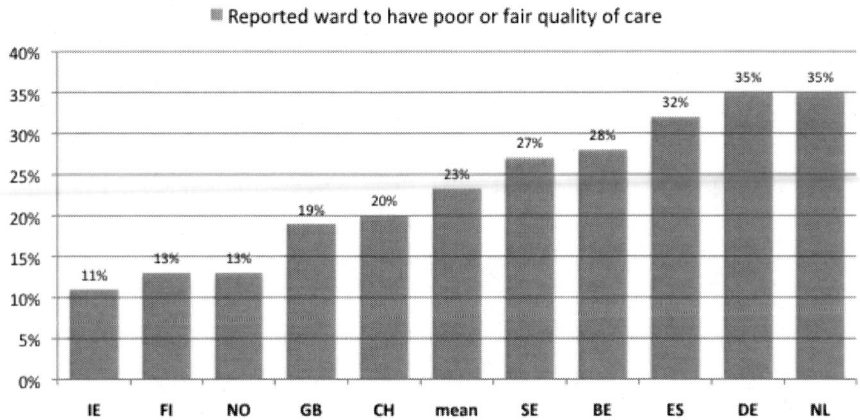

Figure 11. Nurse reports of poor quality of care.

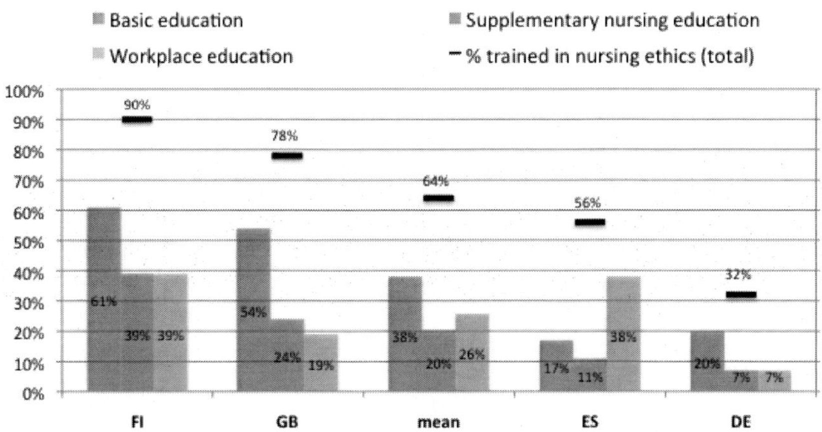

Figure 12. Ethics training among nurses.

Quality of end-of-life care is also partly a function of how well trained caregivers are, and the importance of training in medical ethics (e.g., patient autonomy, patient dignity, etc.) is probably second in importance only to training in medical expertise when it comes to providing good quality care to patients at the end of life. Here again, Finland scores quite well, with substantially more Finnish nurses (90%) reporting that they had training in ethics than nurses elsewhere in Europe (see figure 12; Suhonen, Välimäki, Dassen, et al., 2003).

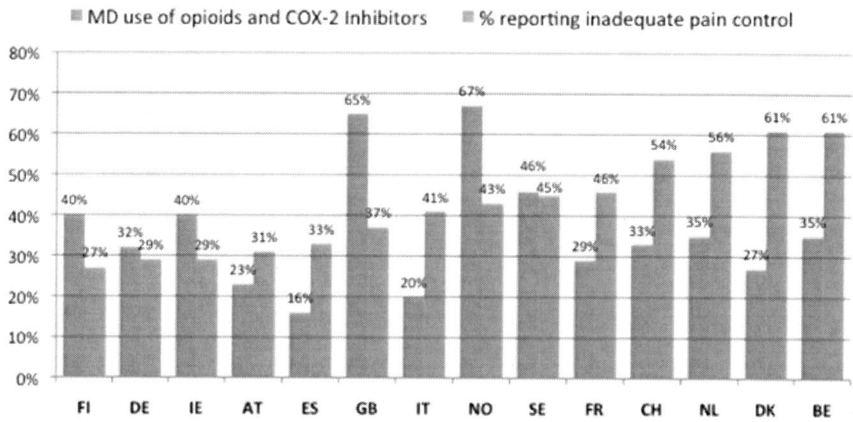

Figure 13. Use of opioids and reports of pain control.

Finland also stands out with regard to treating pain. While Finnish physicians are about "average" when it comes to their willingness to prescribe strong analgesia for pain, Finnish patients report experiencing less inadequate pain control than patients anywhere else in Europe. This result is unlikely to be due to any general predisposition of Scandinavians to accept rather than report their pain, as much higher percentages of patients in Norway (43%), Sweden (45%), and Denmark (61%) reported inadequate pain control (see Figure 13; Breivik).

B. Resource Allocation

While Finland may not devote many resources to end-of-life care in particular, Finland is generally well staffed with medical personnel, overall, scoring better than the UK, Belgium, Spain, and Germany in this regard (see Figure 14; Aiken).

Palliative care training is another key area of concern. As palliative care specialists Poukka (et al.) note, in Finland:

… there are too few specialized palliative care units and too few trained personnel in both specialized palliative care units providing palliative care. Basic education in palliative medicine is not sufficient, and is not well integrated in the education for medical students (Poukka, Korhonen, Pylkkänen, & Saarto, 2010.

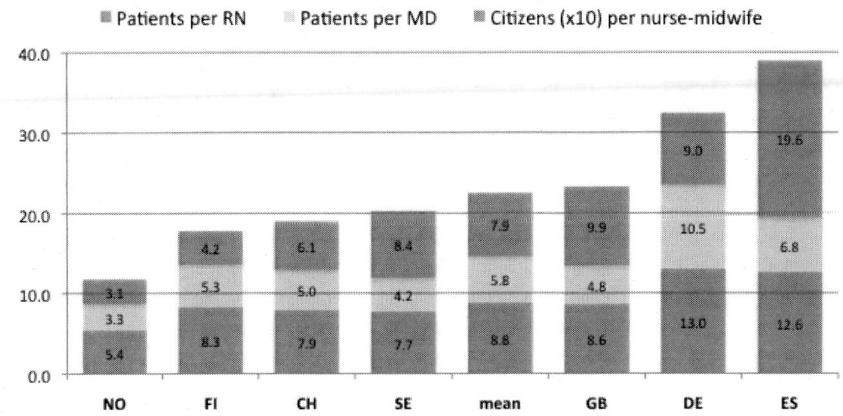

Figure 14. Patient per registered nurse (RN) and medical doctor (MD); nurse/midwives/1k population.

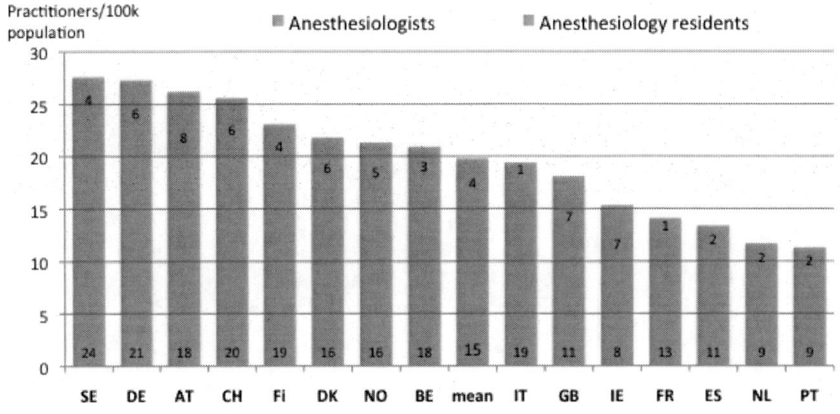

Figure 15. Anaesthesiologists and anaesthesiologist residents per capita.

A study by Centeno (et al.), noting that there are nearly twice as many doctors trained in palliative care per person in the United Kingdom as there are in Finland, seems to underscore this critique (Centeno). At the same time,

Finland scores quite well with regard to the number of anaesthesiologists practicing in its hospitals. As the core speciality from which palliative care first emerged, anaesthesiology is arguably the most important speciality in end-of-life care. And Finland has more anaesthesiologists and anaesthesiology residents per capita (23 per 100,000 population) than most other countries in Europe (see Figure 15; Meeusen, van Zundert, Hoekman, et al., 2010).

Poukka (et al.) also argue that the lack of formal training in palliative care might be partly compensated for by "close collaboration with different associations and organizations involved in end-of-life care in all medical fields in the country" (including more joint local educational events; Poukka). As it turns out, Finnish physicians rank first in Europe in the propensity of its doctors to participate in educational conferences and professional meetings with colleagues. Meanwhile, Sweden ranks a middling ninth, Norway ranks fifteenth, and Denmark ranks last in this regard among the seventeen European countries studied (Burma & Dubois, 2005).

Finally, Poukka (et al.) notes that "research in palliative care is very limited and lacking both intellectual and financial resources" and that reversing this trend is a key to enhancing palliative care in Finland. As it turns out, Finland scores particularly well with regard to research production and financial resources devoted to medical research. In fact, Finland out-performs all countries in Europe except its neighbour to the west: Sweden (see Figure 16).

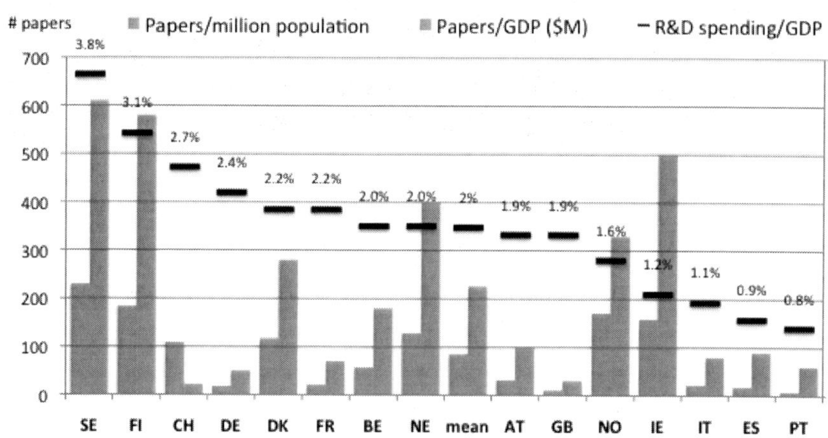

Figure 16. Medical research.

It may well be that more research dollars and hours need to be redeployed to the end-of-life care. But with a robust medical research tradition already in place, the task would appear to be easier in Finland than almost anywhere else in Europe.

Overall, there can be no denying that the quality and accessibility of end-of-life care in Finland and its Nordic neighbours leaves much to be desired. It is argued above that much of the deficit in care can be explained by the role the Scandinavian mindset plays in shaping health care and end-of-life care policies and practices. At the same time, the tradition of good quality care, favourable patient-to-caregiver ratios, and dedication to research all suggest that Finland is well positioned to make gains in the quality of death it provides those within its borders.

REFERENCES

Becker, G., Sarhatlic, R., Olschewski, M., Xander, C., Momm, F. & Blum, H. (2007). 'End-of-Life Care in Hospital'. *Journal of Pain Symptom and Management*, vol. *33*(6), 711-719.

Breivik, H., Cherny, N. & Collett, F. (2009). 'Cancer-related pain: a pan-European survey of prevalence, treatment, and patient attitudes,' *Annals of Oncology*, vol. *20*, 1420–1433.

Breivik, H., Collett, B., Ventafridda, V., Cohen, R. & Gallacher, D. (2006). 'Survey of Chronic Pain in Europe: Prevalence, Impact on Daily Life, and treatment'. *European Journal of Pain*, vol. *10*, 287–333.

Buiting, H., et al. (2007). 'Forgoing Artificial Nutrition or Hydration in Patients Nearing Death in Six European Countries'. *Journal of Pain Symptom Management*, vol. *34*(3), 305-14.

Burma, W. & Dubois, C. (2005). 'Mapping Primary Care Across Europe', in *Primary care in the driver's seat*: R. Saltman, A. Rico, and W. Boerma (eds), Open University Press, Berkshire (UK), 44-45.

Cashman, C. & Slovak, A. (2005). 'The Occupational Medicine Agenda: Routes and Standards of specialization in Occupational Medicine in Europe'. *Occupational Medicine*, vol. *55*, 308–311.

Centeno, C., et al., (2006). *A Map of Palliative Care Specific Resources in Europe*. European Association for Palliative Care (EAPC) Taskforce on the Development of Palliative Care in Europe, Navarra, Spain.

Central Intelligence Agency (CIA). *The World Factbook*. CIA, Washington, 2010.

Cohen, J., et al., (2007). 'End-of-Life Decision-Making in Belgium, Denmark, Sweden and Switzerland: Does Place of Death Make a Difference?' *Journal of Epidemiological Community Health*, vol. *61*, 1062-1068.

Dahl, H. F. (1984). 'Those equal folk'. *Daedalus*, vol. *113*(1), 93-107.

Dickinson, G. & Field, D. (2002). "Teaching End-of-Life Issues: Current Status in U.K. and U.S. Medical Schools." A*merican Journal of Hospice and Palliative Care*, vol. *19*, 181-183.

Dutta, S. (2010). *Global Innovation Index Report 2009-2010.* INSEAD, Fontainebleau (FR), 231, 229, 331.

Economist Intelligence Unit, *The Quality of Death: Ranking End-of-Life Care Across the World.* The Economist, London, 2010.

ESS Round 4: European Social Survey Round 4 Data. (2008). Data file edition 4.0. Norwegian Social Science Data Services, Norway - Data Archive and distributor of ESS data. Retrieved from http://ess.nsd.uib.no/downloadwizard/

European Commission, *European Economic Statistics*. Office for Official Publications of the European Communities, Luxembourg, 2009.

Fearon, J. (2003). 'Ethnic and Cultural Diversity by Country,' *Journal of Economic Growth. 8*, 195-222, 216.

Helliwell, J., Layard, R. & Sachs, J. (2012). *World Happiness Report.* 2012. Columbia University.

Hystad, S. W., Eid, J., Laberg, J., Johnsen, B. H. & Bartone, P. T. (2009). 'Academic stress and health: Exploring the moderating role of personality hardiness,' *Scandinavian Journal of Educational Research*, vol. *53*(5), 21–429.

Inglehart, R. (2010). *World Values Survey.* University of Michigan Institute for Social Research, Ann Arbor (MI).

Levin, T., Li, Y., Weiner, J., Lewis, F., Bartell, A., Piercy, J. & Kissane, D. (2008). 'How Do-Not-Resuscitate Orders Are Utilized in Cancer Patients: Timing Relative to Death and Communication-Training Implications'. *Palliative Support Care*, vol. *6*(4), 341-348.

Löfmark, R., Mortier, F., Nilstun, T., Bosshard, G., Cartwright, C., Van Der Heide, A, Norup, M., Simonato, L. & Onwuteaka-Philipsen, B. (2006). 'Palliative Care Training: A Survey of Physicians in Australia and Europe'. *Journal of Palliative Care*, vol. *22*(2), 105-110.

Los Angeles Times, 'Happiness tops in Denmark, lowest in Togo, study says,' 2 April 2012. Retrieved 17 July 2012. http://latimesblogs.latimes.com/world_now/2012/04/happiness-world-bhutan-meeting-denmark.html

Maltoni, M., Pittureri, C., Scarpi, E., Piccinini, L., Martini, F., Turci, P., Montanari, L., Nanni, O. & Amadori, D. (2009). 'Palliative Sedation Therapy Does Not Hasten Death: Results from a Prospective Multicenter Study'. *Annals of Oncology*, vol. *20*(7), 1163-1169.

Miccinesi, G., Rietjens, J., Deliens, L., Paci, E., Bosshard, G., Nilstun, T., Norup, M. & van der Wal, G. (2006). 'Continuous Deep Sedation: Physicians' Experiences in Six European Countries'. *Journal of Pain Symptom Management*, vol. *31*(2), 122-129.

Ministry of Health and Prevention (DK), *Health Care in Denmark.* Ministeriet for Sundhed og Forebyggelse, Copenhagen, 2008.

Neergaard, M. (2009). *Palliative Home Care for Cancer Patients in Denmark.* University Faculty of Health Sciences, Arhus (DK).

Poukka, P., Korhonen, T., L Pylkkänen, L. & Saarto, T. (2010). 'The Budapest Commitments. The Finnish Association of Palliative Care,' 10 Oct.

Reputation Institute. Which Countries Like Themselves Best, 12. Accessed 23 November 2010.

Rietjens, J., van Delden, J., Onwuteaka-Philipsen, B., Buiting, H., van der Maas, P. & van der Heide, A. (2008). 'Continuous Deep Sedation for Patients Nearing Death in the Netherlands: A Descriptive Study.' *British Medical Journal*, vol. *336*, 810-815.

Sandemose, A. (1936). *A Fugitive Crosses His Tracks*. Knopf, New York,.

Scheier, M. F. & Carver, C. S. (1985). 'Optimism, coping and health: Assessment and implications of generalized outcome expectancies,' *Health Psychology,* vo. *4*, 219-247.

Seal, C. (2009). 'Continuous deep sedation in medical practice: a descriptive study'. *Journal of Pain and Symptom Management*, vol. *39*(1), 44-53.

Social Protection in the European Union. Eurostat: Statistics in Focus 2008. Office for Official Publications of the European Communities, Luxembourg, 2008.

Suhonen, R., Välimäki, M., Dassen, T., et al, (2003). 'Patients' autonomy in surgical care: a comparison of nurses' perceptions in five European countries, *International Nurse Review*, vol. *50*(2), 85-94.

The Solid Facts: Palliative Care, E. Davies and I. Higginson (eds). (2009). WHO Regional Office for Europe, Copenhagen.

van Delden, J., Löfmark, R., Deliens, L., Bosshard, G., Norup, M., Cecioni, R. & van der Heide, A. (2006). 'Do-Not-Resuscitate Decisions in Six European Countries'. *Critical Care Medicine*, vol. *34*(6), 1686-1690.

van der Boom, H. (2008). *Home Nursing in Europe.* Aksant Academic Publishers, Amsterdam, 110 p.

World Health Organization (WHO), *European Health Report 2009*, WHO Regional Office for Europe, Copenhagen, 2009, 15 p.

Wrosch, C., Scheier, M. F. (2003). 'Personality and Quality of Life: The Importance of Optimism and Goal Adjustment,' *Quality of Life Research*, vol. *12*, Supplement: Multidisciplinary Perspectives on Health-Related Quality of Life, 59-72

In: Hospice Care
Editors: J. Hanl and S. Koeck
ISBN: 978-1-62618-456-5

Chapter 3

RENAL CONSIDERATIONS IN PALLIATIVE MEDICINE

Thomas Bui
Kaiser Permanente Hospice and Palliative Medicine
Fellowship Training Program, Portland, OR, US

ABSTRACT

Palliative evaluation and interventions for End Stage Renal Disease (ESRD) are often not systematically implemented for the 400,000 people in the United States on dialysis, which nonetheless maintains a mortality rate of 15 to 20% per year. A significant public health and Medicare policy concern, treating ESRD patients directly costs the United States over $40 billion in public and private funds annually. Although dialysis is life sustaining, patient-physician relationships that emphasize shared decision-making on rational dialysis will maximize quality of life. Patient-centered decisions for the ESRD population, typically on dialysis as destination therapy, must primarily ask whether a patient agrees to the quality of life ramifications of initiating dialysis. Validated prognostic tools, such as the Charleson Comorbidity Index and National Kidney Foundation guidelines, assist patients prioritizing their treatment preferences. Then palliative services must be offered to all ESRD patients who suffer burdens of disease. ESRD standard of care must implement palliative best practices for treatment of uremic pruritis, neuropathy, depression, protein-energy malnutrition, and renal considerations of opioid-based pain management. Rational dialysis – not rationing dialysis

– prescribes an organized plan for the ESRD patient and family to individualize risks and benefits of starting and/or withdrawing dialysis with appropriate hospice support. Using a systematic approach to communicate about diagnosis, prognosis, treatment options, and goals of care is a realistic patient advocacy strategy and restores ESRD patients' dignity at the end of life.

Case Study 1: Mr. K is a 91-yr-old man with CHF, atrial fibrillation (on Coumadin x 5 years), aortic aneurysm, COPD, and Hypertensive CKD Stage 4 acutely exacerbated due to cardiorenal dysfunction. He has a GFR 24 and Creatinine 3.5 as well as documented functional decline (FAST 6). His recent echocardiogram showed Grade III or restrictive diastolic function and severe pulmonary hypertension. over the years, Mr. K's nephrologist had discussions with the patient and his family explaining that the patient was a poor dialysis candidate due to his co-morbidities. According to the Charlson Comorbidity Index (CCI), Mr. K's score is a 10 with 1-year survival probability of 52 ± 9 %. Mr. K's nephrologist, in conjunction with the Palliative Medicine team, focused on the question: "*When to start (or not start) dialysis?*"

Case Study 2: Mrs. M is a 86-yr-old woman with CKD Stage 5 (GFR 9) on hemodialysis (M/W/F) admitted for cholecystitis. Her imaging revealed tumor infiltrating her gallbladder fossa with bowel involvement and anticipated complete bowel obstruction soon. Mrs. M's peritoneal biopsy revealed metastatic ovarian serous carcinoma and peritoneal serous carcinoma complicated by presumed spontaneous bacterial peritonitis. The consultant surgeon indicated that a cholecystostomy tube will not benefit Mrs. M. The consultant oncologist confirmed terminal disease and, after considering the unfavorable benefit-to-burden ratio, offered no chemotherapy for Mrs. M's malignant ascites. Mrs. M's nephrologist, in conjunction with the Palliative Medicine team, focused on the question: "*When to stop dialysis?*"

History and Scope of the Problem

In the 1950's, Hemo-Dialysis (HD) emerged as *"life-saving therapy"* for renal failure. By 1972, the relatively rare HD technology was allocated by *"God committees"* with the intention that HD recipients would be able to return to the workforce. Increased prevalence of HD amongst many patient groups by the 2000's forced the U.S. Congress to modify HD reimbursement through the Composite Bundled Rate. It remains to be seen just how the recently legislated Patient Protection and Affordable Care Act (PPACA) will address ESRD patients' dialysis accessibility in its mandate for chronic disease management as an "essential health benefit." Counter to the initial aim of HD to enable recipients to work, though, more patients are utilizing HD today yet only 20% of these HD patients aged < 55 are employed.

Growing at a rate of 3-4% per year, the HD-dependent population is an emergent factor in the healthcare policy of the United States. In 2009, about 400,000 people initiated hemodialysis as "destination therapy" to treat ESRD. The dialysis population will likely double in size over the next decade with patients > 75 yrs old representing one of the fastest growing segments.

According to the United States Renal Data System, 8.4% of the Medicare population in 2010 had Chronic Kidney Disease (CKD) as estimated using a point prevalent model from their 5 percent Medicare sample. However, these CKD patients accounted for 17% of the annual costs of Medicare patients.

When considering adjusted all-cause mortality in ESRD, patients aged 65+ on dialysis represented slightly more than 300 deaths per 1,000 patient years at risk in 2010.

Although dialysis is life sustaining, these HD patients will nonetheless die with a mortality rate still 15 to 20% per year.

Aware of the longevity compromise expected with ESRD even on HD, then, Palliative Medicine interventions for symptom control and medical decision making seek to optimize quality of life. Balancing the bioethical principles of Autonomy, Non-Beneficence, and Distributive Justice, how do we healthcare providers promote high-quality care for all patients with kidney disease and best discuss starting Palliative Medicine in ESRD?

In April 2011 the American Society of Nephrology (ASN) Quality and Patient Safety Task Force recommended the following guideline consistent with Palliative Medicine tenets:

> "Don't initiate chronic dialysis without ensuring a shared decision-making process between patients, their families, and their physicians."

END STAGE RENAL DISEASE (ESRD) DEFINITION

The presence of kidney damage >3 months defines ESRD according to the ASN.Whereas the normal Glomerular Filtration Rate (GFR) in young adults is 125 mL/min/1.73 m^2, any GFR <15 mL/min/1.73 m^2 is defined as kidney failure.

Albuminuria or GFR <60 mL/min/1.73 m^2 irrespective of cause are key clinical markers for kidney injury.With these readily available objective markers for ESRD, what other tools and techniques can we healthcare providers use when our patients ask if and when to start dialysis?

Prognostication in ESRD

A particular advantage of nephrology is the ability to use readily available biomarkers to monitor symptom onset, categorize diagnosis, and adjust medications.Albuminuria or GFR logbooks, for instance, can objectively assist with refined prognostication.The Charleson Comorbidity Index (CCI) considers ESRD patients' concurrent medical conditions to predict survival.Higher comorbidity in ESRD leading to decreased patient survival may seem intuitive, but quantifying it may be more meaningful for patients.The information the CCI provides is also meaningful for clinicians and patients' families who recognize that HD aims not only at prolonging life, but also at achieving the greatest possible well being and realistic functioning with multiple medical illnesses.

Age, comorbidity, and functional capacity predict survival and morbidity of patients on dialysis.Cohen and colleages (2010) also devised a validated simple instrument to predict 6-month mortality among ESRD patients on HD.This prognostic instrument incorporates 5 simple elements: Age; Serum albumin; Peripheral vascular disease; Dementia; and a Surprise question: "*Would I be surprised if this patient died in the next year?*"

The prognostic utility of monitoring kidney disease progression empowers Primary Care, Nephrology, and Palliative Medicine specialists to collaborate for ESRD patients' ongoing support and education.Ideally such inter-disciplinary teamwork involves ESRD patients prior to periods of instability or declining capacity.Formal assessment of palliative care can then avail ESRD patients to appropriate levels of care and resources in a timely manner.

When to Start Dialysis in ESRD?

The National Kidney Foundation has established the clinical practice guidelines for chronic kidney disease Kidney Disease Outcomes Quality Initiative (KDOQI) for when to start HD.In general, HD is indicated when GFR < 15 mL/min; Kidney function (K_rt/V_{urea} /wk) > 2.0; or Nutritional indices < 0.9 g/kg/day.

Treatment goals should be discussed as soon as possible in the course of a given patient's kidney disease and continue as his or her kidney disease progresses.In the IDEAL Study, Cooper et al studied 828 ESRD patients were studied in 32 centers across Australia and New Zealand to examine whether the timing of the initiation of maintenance dialysis early (GFR of 10-14 mL/min/1.73m^2) versus late (GFR of 5-7mL/min/1.73m^2) influenced survival.No survival advantage was seen for early dialysis, and point estimates for cardiac events actually favored the later start.

This study also suggests that waiting for symptoms to occur and for the patient's body to tell clinicians is acceptable--rather than simply relying on the lab values--for determining the ideal time to start dialysis.Patient-centered decisions for the ESRD population, typically on dialysis as destination therapy, must primarily ask whether a patient even agrees to the quality of life ramifications of initiating dialysis.

In 2010, the Renal Physicians Association (RPA) similarly described quality of life guidelines for shared decision-making in the appropriate initiation of withdrawal from dialysis as follows:

1. Develop a Physician-Patient Relationship for Shared Decision-Making
2. Fully Inform Acute Kidney Injury (AKI), Stage 4 and 5 Chronic Kidney Disease (CKD), and ESRD Patients about Their Diagnosis, Prognosis, and All Treatment Options
3. Give All Patients with AKI, Stage 5 CKD, or ESRD an Estimate of Prognosis Specific to Their Overall Condition
4. Institute Advance Care Planning
5. If Appropriate, Forgo (Withhold Initiation or Withdraw Ongoing) Dialysis for Patients with AKI, CKD, or ESRD in Certain, Well-defined Situations
6. Consider Forgoing Dialysis for AKI, CKD, or ESRD Patients Who Have a Very Poor Prognosis or for Whom Dialysis Cannot Be Provided Safely
7. Consider a Time-Limited Trial of Dialysis for Patients Requiring Dialysis, But Who Have an Uncertain Prognosis, or for Whom a Consensus Cannot Be Reached about Providing Dialysis
8. Establish a Systematic Due Process Approach for Conflict Resolution if There Is Disagreement about What Decision Should Be Made with Regard to Dialysis

9. To Improve Patient-Centered Outcomes, Offer Palliative Care Services and Interventions to All AKI, CKD, and ESRD Patients Who Suffer from Burdens of Their Disease
10. Use a Systematic Approach to Communicate about Diagnosis, Prognosis, Treatment Options, and Goals of Care

These RPA guidelines emphasize quality standards in the decision making and treatment of ESRD.Clinicians must foster good communication with their ESRD patients on the benefits and burdens of initiating dialysis.Healthcare teams and their Palliative Medicine consultants also should document the medical factsand all assessments regarding ESRD diagnosis and prognosis.

Since clinical recommendations on when to start dialysis must be grounded in objective findings, using a systematic approach to communicate about diagnosis and prognosis is pivotal.Conversely, reasons to forgo dialysis must also be rational and take into consideration patients' values since starting HD assumes significant burdens that may detract from these patients' quality of life.

Quality of Life Affected on Dialysis

Dialysis can be life-sustaining but at what cost?Until ESRD patients are routinely going to their routine 4-hour long HD sessions 3 times per week, many of them do not appreciate how significantly their dialysis schedule hampers lifestyle.

Davison (2010) surveyed 584 CKD 4/5 patients about their end-of-life care preferences and perceptions about dialysis and found that 61% regretted their decision to start HD.Whereas most studies assess a limited number of symptoms rather than total symptom burden in ESRD patients, many HD patients reported chronic dialysis itself has associated morbidity.Within the study group, 87% described Fatigue; 75% had Pruritis; and 20% reported Depression.If an individual ESRD patient has overall poor life expectancy, the question of whether or not HD actually extend prognosis becomes even more relevant.In a survey of 3700 nursing home residents across U.S. who started HD, 58% died within 1 year after initiation of HD.Only 13% maintained pre-dialysis function despite the significant resource investment, stress on already debilitated global physiologic reserves, and the logistical burden of thrice weekly HD.The comprehensive aim of Renal Palliative Medicine patients is to simultaneously support nephrology patients and their families throughout the continuum of 1) Symptom Management and 2) Decision Making, especially weighing ESRD patients' quality of life and its potential compromise with HD.

RENAL PALLIATIVE MEDICINE: CLINICAL PEARLS OF SYMPTOM MANAGEMENT

Pain Management in ESRD

Dialysis itself is not painless:50% of patients on dialysis report pain which can be severe and a worse outcome than uremic death.Such pain can be directly dialysis-related, such as abdominal pain in peritoneal dialysis, fistula discomfort, and cramps associated with headaches after dialysis volume flux.Pain is the most frequently reported symptom in the dying patient with chronic kidney disease with 75% of ESRD population describing pain during last week of life.In one study by Cohen (2005) on patients' family perspective of ESRD deaths, 90% reported extremely or moderately severe pain.Home-based, palliative management of renal disease addresses other sources of pain prevalent in and exacerbating the co-morbid ESRD, including vascular disease, arthritis, and immobility as well as existential suffering.As a result, ESRD patients had significantly less likelihood of pain if died at home compared with those who died in an institution.

At the end-of-life, there is no reason for withholding analgesics after regularly reviewing ESRD patients and their needs.Yet total pain can be difficult to treat especially in elderly ESRD patients, and physicians are wary about ESRD drug dosing and toxicity.Furthermore, ESRD patients are often taking multiple other medications and have co-morbid conditions that confound comprehensive pain control.

Note that any drug information provided in this chapter is solely meant as guidelines and therefore must be tailored to the individual patient's clinical scenario, with physician clinical judgment, and consultation with the respective institution's policies and drug formulary.

As a practical guideline for pain management in ESRD, clinicians should use the World Health Organization (WHO) three-step analgesic ladder.Applying the original version of SF-MPQ (McGill Pain Questionnaire) has been used to assess of patients with ESRD leading to effective pain relief in 96% of hemodialysis patients.Barakzoy et al (2006) reviewed the efficacy of this stepwise approach to exclude drugs unsafe in renal failure and concluded that it was validated for ESRD as follows:

Step 1 agents (Mild pain 1-4): Use acetaminophen, which is safe in renal failure, but do not exceed 4000 mg per day to avoid iatrogenic hepatotoxicity. Adjuvant pain medications include neuropathic agents and Non-Steroidal Anti-Inflammatory Drugs (NSAID's), which often need dose modification in ESRD.

Step 2 agents (Moderate pain 5-6): Use codeine, which has a significantly increased half-life in renal failure. Tramadol is safe and effective, but generally needs 50% dose reduction.

Step 3 agents (Severe pain 7-10): Chronic use of all opioids needs close monitoring. Anecdotal evidence suggests less toxicity with Hydromorphone (Dilaudid) orally as well as Fentanyl and alfentanil delivered parentally (subcutaneously).

An alternate tiered approach for pain management in ESRD is based on the relative safety of each opioid medication in this population.Initial dosing of the safer opioids in renal failure is based on Creatinine Clearance with normal dosing if Creatine Clearance > 50 mL/min but dose generally decreased 50% if Creatine Clearance < 10 mL/min.The following categories reflect opioid metabolites' safety profiles in ESRD:

Not Recommended for Use: Meperidine is not recommended due to accumulation of the metabolite normeperidine, which can cause seizures. Codeine should be avoid in patients with GFR <30 mL/min can cause profound toxicity may be delayed and occur after only trivial doses. Dextropropoxyphene is not recommended for use in patients with ESRD because it is associated with central nervous system (CNS) and cardiac toxicity. Morphine is not recommended for chronic use if GFR <30 mL/min due to rapid accumulation of active, neurotoxic, non-dialyzable metabolites. Morphinemetabolites, morphine-3-glucuronide and morphine-6-glucuronide, may lead to myoclonic jerks. If morphine must be used, avoid long-acting preparations and monitor closely for toxicity.

Use with Caution: Oxycodone should be used cautiously in ESRD since, though it is metabolized in the liver, 19% is excreted unchanged in the urine. Therefore, accumulation of the parent compound and metabolites in renal failure can lead to CNS toxicity and sedation. Hydromorphone (parent drug) does not substantially accumulate in HD patients, but Hydromorphone-3-glucuronide (active metabolite) quickly accumulates between dialysis treatments; it appears to be effectively removed during hemodialysis so with careful monitoring may be used safely in dialysis patients. Hydromorphone should be used cautiously in patients with a GFR < 30mL/min who have yet to start dialysis or who have withdrawn from dialysis. Avoid chronic Demerol (meperidine) since the normeperidine metabolite accumulates and can lead to CNS excitability and seizures.

*Safest in Renal Insufficiency:*Fentanyl has no active metabolites, and most studies do not show drug accumulation of this non-dialyzable drug that has both high protein binding and a high volume of distribution.Transdermal fentanyl is particularly useful when ESRD pain is chronic and stable; it is helpful if the ESRD patient can tolerate a dose of strong opioid equivalent to 60–120 mg of oral morphine/24h. Methadone is also considered safe in ESRD since it has no active metabolites and low plasma accumulation due to its enhanced fecal elimination.Methadone does not appear to be removed by dialysis and is a good option for ESRD neuropathic pain.

Constipation

Decreased frequency of bowel movements almost invariably occurs with the use of opiates. It judicious to prescribe any of the following bowel regimens as soon as any opioid pain medication is started in ESRD patients:

- Docusate 100 mg PO twice daily
- Senna 8.6 mg take 2 tabs PO BID
- Lactulose (10 g/15 mL syrup) 15 to 30 mL PO daily
- Bisacodyl 30 mg PO or 10 mg PR supp once daily
- Saline enemas or glycerine rectal suppositories
- Osmotic: Fleets®; Miralax®
- Bulk: Bran 20 g/day; Metamucil®

Neuropathic Myoclonus

Muscle twitching is a ESRD symptom that can be anticipated and treated to alleviate the suffering of the patient and distress such spasms cause family members.When myclonus is uremic-associated, it may be treated with benzodiazepines.Muscle twitching in ESRD may also be iatrogenic due to Morphine metabolites (morphine-3-glucuronide and morphine-6-glucuronide), which may lead to myoclonic jerks.In this case, the opioid dose may need to be decreased or substituted altogether.

Seizures develop in <10% of patients who withdraw from dialysis so routine, prophylactic anticonvulsants are not recommended.

Protein-Energy Malnutrition

Malnutrition is common in ESRD due to decreased intestinal absorption, digestion, and metabolic acidosis.Endocrine disorders of uremia, such as insulin resistance and hyperparathyroidism, can also be anticipated and treated with dietician expertise.According to the U.S. 3rd Nat'l Health and Nutrition Survey (NHANES), age ≥60 years and GFR <30 mL/min were independently associated with malnutrition.Researchers also found a strong correlation between malnutrition and death in maintenance dialysis patients.

Mindful of the accumulation of endogenously formed uremic toxins that affect ESRD protein-energy malnutrition, an ESRD Palliative Medicine goal is to monitor nutritional status as reflected in low Protein Equivalent of Total Nitrogen Appearance normalized to body weight (nPNA).Since creatinine varies with muscle mass as well as GFR, we must pay attention to surrogate nutrition parameters, such as pre-dialysis Albumin (goal 4.0 g/dL by bromcresol green method).Other simple, low-cost anthropometric markers of protein-energy nutritional status can be followed chronologically in ESRD patients as follows:

- Percent of usual body weight
- Body Mass Index (BMI)
- Mid-arm muscle circumference
- Subjective global assessment
- Dietary interviews and diaries

Pruritus

Uremia in ESRD causes pruritis; this distressing sequelacan be evaluated and treated.Excoriations and cutaneous superinfection are risks that can be avoided with anticipatory guidance from Palliative Medicine specialists.Some treatment regimens for uremia-induced pruritis cited in the literature are as follows:

Naltrexone 50 mg PO daily for 4 weeks: This µ-receptor antagonist is particularly helpful if the ESRD patient does not report concomitant pain symptoms. Nine of 23 patients complained about GI side events.

Tacrolimus 0.03% oint Apply topically BID to areas most affected for 7 days: Potentially carcinogenic if systemically administered. Use with caution in treating patients over longer periods.

Gabapentin 200mg PO 3 times per week after HD: This drug has a longer half-life in patients on hemodialysis. Therefore, ESRD patients may need lower doses at less frequent intervals.

Other anti-pruritic treatment options: Sarna® and other topically applied menthol lotions; Benadryl® and other anti-histamines; Ultraviolet therapy; Oral activated charcoal; and Electric needle acupuncture.

Renal Palliative Medicine: Supporting Patients' Values

Adopting a shared decision making model of care in advanced kidney disease necessitates healthcare professionals actively listening and dedication to patient choice in renal failure.Understanding each patient's values and how they learn and make choices improvements their experience of care and fosters better clinical outcomes.Integrating treatment preferences deliberately considers of risks and benefits and individualized medical decision-making based on medical co-morbidities and overall ESRD disease burden, especially when to start (or not start) HD and when to discontinue it.

Thoughtful withdrawal of dialysis is not euthanasia.In this setting, symptoms related to the accumulation of toxins and fluid can be anticipated and managed.The uremic death can be anticipated approximately 10 days after maintenance HD withdrawal and is characterized as painless when managed by Renal Palliative Medicine techniques.Pharmacological intervention of uremic symptoms as well as expert management of pain from non-renal comorbid disease is of paramount importance.Clinicians must be attuned to the impact of renal failure on the excretion of various drugs and their metabolites upon withdrawal of dialysis.

Clinicians must also logically weigh out competing ESRD treatment decisions (e.g., by prioritizing the kidney transplant evaluation, there may be less time for home dialysis training).In this clinician-patient partnership, patients have a responsibility to prioritize outcomes that matter to them and verbalize those preferences.Clinical practice guidelines for ESRD care traditionally have taken an age-neutral approach that allow clinicians flexibility to adapt them.Accordingly, nephrology fellowship training programs have undertaken the responsibility to engage trainees in Renal Palliative Medicine topics.

Lack of education and training of the medical team need for end-of-life care training in nephrology has highlighted some barriers to Renal Palliative Medicine.Fear of ‘getting it wrong’ can paralyze clinicians such that they fail to identify ESRD patients whose multiple medical co-morbidities may not benefit from hemodialysis; such reluctance may preclude thoroughly explaining non-HD options.Strengthening partnerships with Primary Care Physicians leverages their long-term patient care relationships with mutual ESRD patients to help synthesize a common language between healthcare professionals.

Improved communication thus puts ESRD patients’ healthcare providers on the same page for a cohesive treatment plan consistent with the individual patient’s preferences.At present, ESRD patients are referred late in the dying process. The length of hospice enrollment for ESRD patients is on average only 14 days while for other diseases, the average is 59 days.Quality improvement initiatives in communication of Palliative ESRD care advocate for quality benchmarks, such as quantifying how nephrologists communicate with palliative medicine specialists and continually asking: “*How does my patient prioritize quality of life?*”

CONCLUSION

One of the major goals of the Healthy People 2020 (HP2020) public health program is to “reduce new cases of CKD and its complications, disability, death, and economic costs” in the United States.Directly advancing that HP2020 goal, the clinical ESRD expertise of Palliative Medicine specialists is the education of both patient and family on the natural history of kidney disease and overall prognosis. Accordingly, the Palliative Medicine community agrees with ASN Quality and Patient Safety Task Force’s recommendation to ensure a shared decision-making process between patients, their families, and their physicians when starting or stopping dialysis.

Clarifying realistic expectations and treatment options synergistically achieves patient and family comfort. Renal palliative care thus incorporates communication of prognosis, advance care planning, and symptom assessment and management to improve not only patients' quality of life, but also quality of dying.Palliative Medicine specialists must strive to help their Nephrology colleagues provide clinical resources and psycho-social support for both patients and their loved ones.

Rational dialysis – not rationing dialysis – prescribes an organized plan for the ESRD patient and family to individualize risks and benefits of starting and/or withdrawing dialysis with appropriate hospice support by mobilizing community agencies.

The option of *not* initiating dialysis must be explicit if it is futile or even detrimental, but it also must include a systematic plan for supporting the patient and his or her family.Limiting the use of dialysis therapy in such circumstances balances the bioethical principles of Autonomy, Non-Beneficence, and Distributive Justice in ESRD.

As healthcare providers who promote high-quality care for all patients with kidney disease, we must inculcate teamwork with Primary Care Physicians, Nephrologists, and Palliativists to fully supports patients and answer their questions.

On the individual level, treating ESRD substantially improves a patient's quality of life. Improving ESRD patients' quality of life encompasses renal considerations of opioid-based pain regimens and management of uremic pruritis, neuropathy, depression, and protein-energy malnutrition.Conservative management that aims to improve ESRD patients' total quality of life by expertly anticipating then treating uremic symptoms is indeed the ESRD Palliative Medicine standard of excellence.

Together we can meet the large unmet need to alleviate the physical, psychosocial, and existential suffering of patients with ESRD. Consistent with RPA guidelines, we must offer palliative services to all AKI, CKD, and ESRD patients who suffer burdens of disease.

Prognostic tools and other clinical practice guidelines are readily available to assist patient-centered clinicians incorporating palliative care into ESRD management.Palliative care in the ESRD population in its simplest sense is anticipating practical symptoms based on uremic physiology and staying ahead of the patient's needs—in his or her biologic, psychological, social, and spiritual spheres.

References

Barakzoy AS, Moss AH.Efficacy of the world health organization analgesic ladder to treat pain in end-stage renal disease. *J. Am. Soc. Nephrol.* 2006;17(11):3198.

Boyd CM, Darer J, Boult C *et al.* Clinical practice guidelines and quality of care for older patients with multiple comorbid diseases: implications for pay for performance. *JAMA* 2005; 294: 716–724.

Chandra SM, Shulz J, Lawrence C, Greenwood RN, Farrington K. Is there a rationale for rationing chronic dialysis? A hospital based cohort study of factors affecting survival and morbidity. *Br Med J* 1999; 318: 217–223.

Cohen LM, Germain MJ, Woods AL, Mirot A, Burleson JA. The family perspective of ESRD deaths.*Am. J .Kidney Dis.* 2005;45(1):154.

Cohen LM, Ruthazer R, Moss AH, Germain MJ. Predicting six-month mortality for patients who are on maintenance hemodialysis. *Clin. J. Am. Soc. Nephrol.*2010; 5:72–79.

Cooper BA, Branley P, Bulfone L, et al. A randomized, controlled trial of early versus late initiation of dialysis. *N Engl J Med.* 2010;363:609-619.

Davison SN. End of life care preferences and needs: perceptions of patients with chronic kidney disease. *Clin. J. Am. Soc. Nephrol.* 2010 Feb;5(2):195-204.

Gianni LM, Sulli MM. Topical tacrolimus in the treatment of atopic dermatitis. *Ann. Pharmacother.*2001; 35: 943–946.

Gunal A, et al. Gabapentin therapy for pruritus in haemodialysis patients: a randomized, placebo-controlled, double-blind trial. *Nephrol. Dial. Transplant* 2004 Dec;19(12):3137-9.

Holley JL, Carmody SS, Moss AH et al. The need for end-of-life care training in nephrology: national survey results of nephrology fellows. *Am. J. Kidney Dis.*2003; 42: 813–820.

Kurella Tamura M, Cohen LM. Should there be an expanded role for palliative care in end-stage renal disease? *Curr. Opin. Nephrol. Hypertens.* 2010 Nov; 19(6):556-60.

Kurella Tamura M, et al. Functional status of elderly adults before and after Initiation of dialysis. *NEJM* 2009; 361:1539-1547.

Merkus MP, Jager KJ, Dekker FW, de Haan RJ, Boeschoten EW, Krediet RT. Physical symptoms and quality of life in patient on chronic dialysis: results of the Netherlands cooperative study on adequacy of dialysis (NECOSAD). *Nephrol. Dial Transplant.*1999; 14:1163–1170.

Neely KJ, Roxe DM. Palliative care/hospice and the withdrawal of dialysis. *J. Palliat. Med.* 2000;3(1):57.

O'Hare AM, Rodriguez RA, Hailpern SM *et al.* Regional variation in health care intensity and treatment practices for end-stage renal disease in older adults. *JAMA*2010; 304: 180–186.

Pauli-Magnus C, Mikus G, Alscher DM et al. Naltrexone does not relieve uremic pruritus: results of a randomized, placebo-controlled crossover-study. *J. Am. Soc. Nephrol.*2000; 11: 514–519.

Peer G, Kivity S, Agami O et al. Randomised crossover trial of naltrexone in uraemic pruritus. *Lancet* 1996; 348: 1552–1554.

Pisoni RL, Wikstrom B, Elder SJ et al. Pruritus in haemodialysis patients: international results from the Dialysis Outcomes and Practice Patterns Study (DOPPS). *Nephrol. Dial Transplant.*2006; 21: 3495–3505.

Shared decision-making in the appropriate initiation of withdrawal from dialysis. 2nd ed. Rockville (MD): Renal Physicians Association (RPA); 2010 Oct. p. 39-92.

Song MK, et al. Randomized controlled trial of SPIRIT: an effective approach to preparing African-American dialysis patients and families for end of life. *Res. Nurs Health.* 2009;32(3):260.

Swartz R, Perry E, Daley J. The frequency of withdrawal from acute care is impacted by severe acute renal failure. *J. Palliat. Med.* 2004 Oct; 7(5):676-82.

U.S. Renal Data System, USRDS 2012 Annual Data Report: Atlas of End-Stage Renal Disease in the United States, National Institutes of Health, National Institute of Diabetes and Digestive and Kidney Diseases, Bethesda, MD, 2012.

http://www.eperc.mcw.edu/EPERC/FastFactsIndex/ff_161.htm

http://www.guidelines.gov/content.aspx?id=24176andsearch=dialysis

http://www.kidney.org/professionals/kdoqi/pdf/KDOQI2000NutritionGL.pdf

http://www.usrds.org/reference.aspx

In: Hospice Care
Editors: J. Hanl and S. Koeck

ISBN: 978-1-62618-456-5

Chapter 4

USING EVIDENCE-BASED MEASURES TO DOCUMENT DECLINE IN HOSPICE PATIENTS: REGULATION MEETS CLINICAL PRACTICE

***William D. Cabin*[1,*] *and Susan Havens Lang*[2]**
[1]Social Work and Gerontology, Richard Stockton College, NJ, US
[2]United Hospice of Rockland, New City, NY, US

ABSTRACT

Hospices have been implementing various approaches to cope with the increased regulatory scrutiny in the last five years, prompted by concern about costs and outcomes. Medicare has increased demands on hospices: enacting more demanding participation criteria in 2008; new mandatory quality data collection and public reporting requirements beginning in 2012; and, through its fiscal intermediaries, more restrictive Local coverage determination (LCD) guidelines for initial and ongoing patient eligibility criteria. This chapter examines how one New York State hospice, ABC hospice, designed a multi-faceted program to simultaneously improve regulatory compliance and improve patient quality of life (QOL). This chapter presents how evidence-based scales in four patient outcome areas (i.e., pain, breathing, functional decline, and anxiety) were developed, implemented and the preliminary evaluation of

[*] Corresponding Author: William D. Cabin: williamcabin@yahoo.com.

results. The chapter helps inform hospices implementing public reporting and other regulatory compliance coping strategies consistent with appropriate clinical practice.

Keywords: Medicare, hospice, documentation, evidence-based practice, functional performance assessments

INTRODUCTION

The purpose of this chapter is to explore the impact of increased regulatory requirements on managing hospice clinical practice.

The Medicare Hospice Benefit has grown significantly since its inception in 1983, serving nearly 1.6 million patients in 2010, with Medicare annual expenditures over $13 billion compared to $3 billion in 2000 [Medicare Payment Advisory Commission (Med Pac), 2011] [National Hospice and Palliative Care Organization (NHPCO), 2011]. Hospice care originally focused on improving cancer patients' end-of-life (EOL) quality of life (QOL) and reducing Medicare's EOL costs (Gage, Miller, Coppola, Harvell, Laliberte, Mor, and Teno, 2000). However, by 2002 non-cancer diagnoses superseded cancer as the primary diagnosis for those served by hospice programs nationwide. In 2010, cancer admissions to hospice constituted 35.6% of all admissions while non-cancer diagnoses were 64.4% of all admissions (NHPCO, 2011). Of the non-cancer diagnoses, heart disease (14.3%), debility unspecified (13%), and dementia (13%), including Alzheimer's disease, were the top diagnoses (NHPCO, 2011). In addition to rising costs and expanding qualifying conditions, Med Pac (2011) has expressed concern about the increased proportion of hospices which are for-profit (from 20% in 2000 to 67% in 2010) and increased profit margins (from 5% in 2004 to 7.5% in 2010).

In response to this trend and overall governmental concern about costs and outcomes, Medicare has increased regulatory requirements steadily since 2007. The first change was in 2008 with the first revision of the Medicare hospice Conditions of Participation (COPs) in 25 years. The new COPs mandated hospices develop and implement Quality Assurance Performance Improvement (QAPI) programs. However, no public reporting of QAPI outcomes was required; nor was there a mandated uniform national assessment instrument and reporting. About the same time, Medicare, through its fiscal intermediaries, issued more restrictive separate Local Coverage Determination

(LCD) guidelines for qualifying criteria for hospice patients admitted for a diagnosis of dementia, Alzheimer's disease (dementia), general decline, heart disease, stroke, liver disease, HIV, ALS, and pulmonary disease, as well as cancer (The Corridor Group, 2008). Medicare fiscal intermediaries simultaneously increased their focus on documentation of LCD guidelines. Effective January 11, 2011, Medicare mandated new certification and recertification requirements, mandating that a physician or nurse practitioner must complete a face-to-face certification of every hospice patient at six months after admission and every 60 days thereafter.

The most recent requirements are in Section 3004 of the Affordable Care Act and detailed in new regulations in the July 13, 2012 Federal Register (NHPCO, 2012). The new law and regulations mandate that hospices collect and publicly report specific quality data. The reporting began voluntarily for a structural measure and patient care measures for October 1-December 31, 2011, with 924 hospices submitting data (Pratt, 2012). The first mandated data collection period was October 1-December 31, 2012 for a structural measure category (with three measures) and a National Quality Forum (NQF) endorsed comfortable dying measure (NQF 209). Structural measure data must be submitted by January 31, 2013; NQF 209 by April 1, 2013, and thereafter will be publicly available on a Center for Medicare and Medicaid Services (CMS) website. Data collection is next mandated for calendar year 2013, with public reporting for both the structural measure category and NQF 209, and annually thereafter.

Effective October 1, 2013, a 2% market basket reduction in payment rates will be imposed on hospices failing to participate in the mandatory collection and submission/reporting requirements (NHPCO, 2012). During the federal fiscal year 2014, which begins October 1, 2013, reporting requirements will include two measurement categories for data collected October 1 – December 31, 2012 (NHPCO, 2012; Pratt, 2012). One is the NQF 209 (comfortable dying measure) which reports on the percentage of a hospice's patients who report being uncomfortable due to pain on the initial assessment (after hospice admission) and who report pain was brought to a comfort level within forty-eight (48) hours. The second measure category is the structural category. To meet the structural requirement hospices must report: whether they participate in a QAPI program, as required; whether the QAPI program has a least three (3) indicators related to patient care; and must check on a list all patient care topics for which they have a QAPI indicator (NHPCO 2012; Pratt 2012).

CMS has not prescribed patient care indicators to date. However, in the preamble to the 2008 QAPI regulation CMS recommended patient care might include: patient self-determination (i.e., patient preference for hospitalization; CPR); comfort (i.e., pain management); safety (i.e., caregiver skills; family confidence in providing safe care); and effective grieving (i.e., caregiver emotional support preparing for death and then coping with death) (Ross, 2011). There also have been reports that CMS and others are recommending hospices use the Hospice and Palliative Care AIM (Assessment, Intervention, Measurement) Project) and the PEACE (Prepare, Embrace, Attend, Communicate, Empower) measures they tested for guidance in developing patient care indicators (Ross, 2011). NHPCO (2012) reports CMS is evaluating whether to mandate data collection and reporting on other NQF measures beginning in 2015, including NQF 1617 (Patients Treated with an Opiod Who Are Given a Bowel Regime); NQF 1634 (Pain Screening); NQF 1637 (Pain Screening); NQF 1638 (Dyspnea Treatment); and NQF 1639 (Dyspnea Screening). Any such additional requirements require new proposed federal regulations.

THE CASE STUDY

Hospices have been implementing various approaches to cope with the increased regulatory scrutiny. We discuss the case of one hospice, Hospice ABC, located in New York State, which designed and implemented a program to simultaneously improve patient quality of life (QOL) and increase compliance with the 2007-2008 QAPI, COP, and LCD requirements. ABC's experience helps inform other hospices addressing similar requirements and the new mandated quality data collection and reporting requirements.

COMPLIANCE PROGRAM EVOLUTION

ABC is a state-licensed, Medicare and Medicaid–certified and Joint Commission (JC) accredited, freestanding non-profit hospice. ABC has an average daily census of 110 patients and an annual budget of $9 million, 90% of which is Medicare. In 2008, approximately 47% of all admitted patients were admitted for a cancer diagnosis with the remaining non-cancer population dominated by End Stage Heart disease (19%), Alzheimer's disease (dementia) (9%), and End Stage Pulmonary disease (COPD/respiratory failure) (7%).

In January 2008, ABC's fiscal intermediary issued a new, more restrictive set of LCDs. At the same time, increased focused medical reviews began focusing on documentation of the non-cancer hospice diagnoses. In June 2008, the draft new Medicare Hospice COP eligibility and QAPI sections indicated that quality measurement was essential in all aspects of care. As a result, ABC decided to design a new set of documentation requirements to ensure better measurement of patient QOL status and compliance with LCD and other regulatory requirements. The program targeted four symptoms: functional decline, anxiety, pain level, and breathing. These symptoms represented symptoms prevalent in almost all hospice patients.

The overall program design was to select evidence-based instruments that would give a baseline measure for each patient and then an ongoing measure of improvement. Furthermore, the instruments facilitated recertification, discharge, and other interdisciplinary team decision-making, as well as to enhance daily interdisciplinary communication. Nursing, social workers, spiritual care practitioners, music and massage therapists' implemented the measures on all direct care visits. As a result of a literature review, ABC selected two new measures to document functional decline; two for pain and one each for anxiety, breathing, and pain.

The program began in July 2008. The program's kick off was an educational program for clinical staff and managers. The goals were to: (1) introduce how to utilize the new instruments for documentation of the specific symptoms; (2) introduce how to use instrument results over time to make patient care decisions; and (3) improve the efficiency and efficacy of documentation. The clinician feedback on the educational program was successful, with clinicians feeling that the new instruments would assist them in accurately documenting patient changes. ABC modified their electronic medical record progress note for each discipline to include new, mandatory fields required by the instruments.

The Instruments

Functional Decline: The Functional Assessment Staging Tool (FAST)

Two instruments were selected to measure functional decline: The Palliative Performance Scale (PPS), to measure decline across various diseases, and the Functional Assessment Staging Tool (FAST), to measure decline in patients with Alzheimer's disease.

FAST (Reisberg, 1988) was selected for two reasons. First, the literature review indicated that FAST is limited as a prognosis instrument, but it is valid and reliable as a measure of decline in dementia patients (Doberman, Yasar and Durso, 2007; Hanrahan, Raymond, McGowen and Luchins, 1999; Luchins, Hanrahan and Murphy, 1997; Schonwetter et al., 2003). Second, NGS recommended its use and actually identified a minimum FAST score for dementia patients to qualify for hospice services. FAST uses a 7-step system to measure functional decline, as illustrated in Table One.

Table 1. Functional Assessment Staging of Alzheimer's Disease (FAST)

Stage	Skill Level
1.	No difficulties, either subjectively or objectively.
2.	Complains of forgetting location of objects. Subjective word findings difficulties.
3.	Decreased job function evident to co-workers; difficulty in traveling to new locations. Decreased organizational capacity.*
4.	Decreased ability to perform complex tasks (e.g., planning dinner for guests), handling personal finances (forgetting to pay bills), difficulty marketing, etc.
5.	Requires assistance in choosing proper clothing to wear for day, season, and occasion.
6a.	Difficulty putting clothing on properly without assistance.
6b.	Unable to bathe properly; (e.g., difficulty adjusting bath water temperature) occasionally or more frequently over the past weeks.*
6c.	Inability to handle mechanics of toileting (e.g., forgets to flush the toilet, does not wipe properly or properly dispose of toilet tissue) occasionally or more frequently over the past weeks.*
6d.	Urinary incontinence, occasional or more frequent.
6e.	Fecal Incontinence, (occasional or more frequently over the past week).
7a.	Ability to speak limited to approximately a half dozen different words or fewer, in the course of an average day or in the course of an intensive interview.
7b.	Speech ability limited to the use of a single intelligible word in an average day or in the course of an interview (the person may repeat the word over and over)
7c.	Ambulatory ability lost (cannot walk without personal assistance)
7d.	Ability to sit up without assistance lost (e.g., the individual will fall over if there are no lateral rests[arms] on the chair)
7e.	Loss of the ability to smile.

* Scored primarily on the basis of information obtained from a knowledgeable informant and/or caregiver.

1984 by Barry Reisberg, M.D. All right reserved. Reisberg, B. Functional Assessment Staging (FAST). Psychopharmacology Bulletin. 1988:24:653-659.

Functional Decline: Palliative Performance Scale (PPS)

PPS was selected for two reasons. First, the literature review indicated the PPS score would document the trajectory of functional decline over the course of the patient's life limiting illness.

Table 2. Palliative Performance Scale (PPSv2) Version 2

PPS Level	Ambulation	Activity and Evidence of Disease	Self-Care	Intake	Conscious Level
100%	Full	Normal activity and work No evidence of disease	Full	Normal	Full
90%	Full	Normal activity and work Some evidence of disease	Full	Normal	Full
80%	Full	Normal activity *with* Effort Some evidence of disease	Full	Normal or reduced	Full
70%	Reduced	Unable Normal Job/Work Significant disease	Full	Normal or reduced	Full
60%	Reduced	Unable hobby/house work Significant disease	Occasional assistance necessary	Normal or reduced	Full or Confusion
50%	Mainly Sit/Lie	Unable to do any work Extensive disease	Considerable assistance required	Normal or reduced	Full or Confusion
40%	Mainly in Bed	Unable to do most activity Extensive disease	Mainly assistance	Normal or reduced	Full or Drowsy +/- Confusion
30%	Totally BedBound	Unable to do any activity Extensive disease	Total Care	Normal or reduced	Full or Drowsy +/- Confusion
20%	Totally BedBound	Unable to do any activity Extensive disease	Total Care	Minimal to sips	Full or Drowsy +/- Confusion
10%	Totally BedBound	Unable to do any activity Extensive disease	Total Care	Mouth care only	Drowsy or Coma +/- Confusion
0%	Death	-	-	-	-

Source: Anderson, Fern et al. (1996) Palliative Performance Scale (PPS) a new tool. *Journal of Palliative Care* 12(1), 5-11. Copyright © 2001 and reprinted with permission of Victoria Hospice Society. Must be used only with instructions and definitions at http://web.his.uvic.ca/Research/NET/tools/PrognosticTools/PalliativePerformanceScale/PPSInstrument.php.

The PPS measurement process is a reliable and valid tool and correlates with survival times for cancer patients (Anderson, 1996; Morita, 1999; and Virik, 2002). Second, ABC's fiscal intermediary had identified in four different LCD guidelines the baseline PPS percentage for appropriateness for hospice eligibility.

The Palliative Performance Scale (PPS) is a modification of the Karnofsky Performance Scale for evaluating functional decline patients requiring palliative, end of life care (Karnofsky, 1948; Anderson, 1996; Virik, 2002; Morita, 1999; Morita, 2000). PPS measures the functional status of a patient and assigns a numerical value based on their abilities in the trajectory of illness (see further, Table Two). PPS uses five practitioner rated domains (ambulation, activity level/evidence of disease, self-care, intake, and level of consciousness). The practitioner scores each domain based on the patient's actual functional ability level. Then the person conducting the visual assessment determines the PPS percent that most accurately represents the patient's abilities. PPS also serves as a communication tool for quickly describing a patient's current level of functional abilities across disciplines.

All ABC professional staff (i.e., nurses, social workers, spiritual care practitioners, and music, massage, and other therapists) utilize PPS to assess each patient's functional ability on each visit. The results are documented in the patient record. This facilitates team collaboration because every team member has a common measure and understanding of the patient's status. As a result, both PPS and FAST enhance ABC's compliance with both Medicare and JC interdisciplinary collaboration requirements. PPS also facilitates documentation of progressive decline to establish continued eligibility documentation for compliance with payer claim processing and auditing requirements. ABC's Interdisciplinary Team (IDT) also uses this score as one concrete measure in determining a patient's care plan changes (if any) and recertification or discharge eligibility. The nurse and other practitioners compare the trajectory of patient scores on functional decline from admission to the current decision-making point.

Pain

Pain-rating scales are used frequently by hospices and other health care facilities because of regulatory and nursing focus on pain management. ABC had been using the McCafferty (1999) linear pain rating scale in the nursing progress notes for several years. The scale rates pain on a "0" to "10" scale with '0' meaning no pain and '10' meaning unbearable pain (McCafferty, 1999) as displayed at the top of Table Three. However, in thinking through the newly revised COP requirements, ABC decided to add additional scales so pain measurement would be more representative of the patient population. Two additional scales were selected for use, based on the individual patient's capabilities. One new scale allows the patient to choose the face that best describes how they feel. This scale is a series of six faces, from a smiley face to a tearful, frowning face (Wong-Baker, 2005). The full smiley face indicates 'no hurt' and the tearful frown indicated 'hurt worst" (See further, bottom of Table Three).

Table 3. Pain Scale

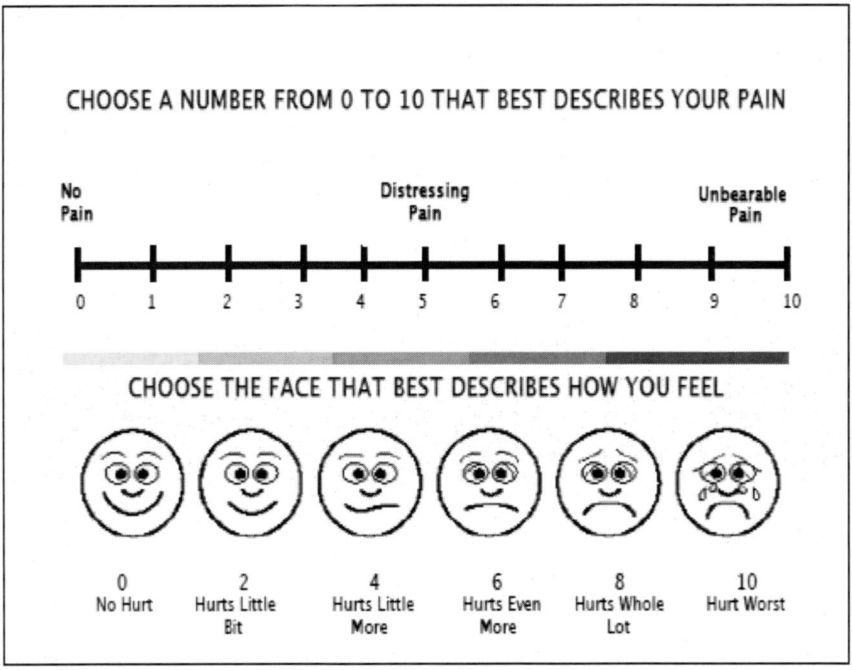

Source: Adapted from Wong-Baker, 2005 and McCafferty, M., and Pasero, C., 1999.

The second new scale is the Pain Assessment in Advanced Dementia (PAINAD) scale (Horgas and Miller, 2008). This scale relies on the practitioner to observe the patient's non-verbal behaviors for five indicators of pain. The practitioner scores each indicator and adds them to establish a total score on a scale of "0" to "10". Zero indicates no pain and a score of 10 indicates severe pain (see further, Table Four).

ABC decided that the clinical staff needed the three scales to most accurately assess and document pain in the end-of-life (EOL) patient population, especially since many of our patients are non-verbal somewhere in their trajectory of illness. Additionally, these three variations could be easily implemented across all disciplines, readily documented and clearly described the individuals level of pain.

Table 4. Pain Assessment in Advance Dementia (PAINAD) Scale - Non-verbal Patients

Items	0	1	2	Score
Breathing independent of vocalization	Normal	Occasional labored breathing. Short period of hyperventilation	Noisy labored breathing, Long period of hyperventilation Cheyne-Stokes respirations	
Negative vocalization	None	Occasional moan or groan, Low level speech with a negative or disapproving quality.	Repeated troubled calling out. Loud moaning or groaning, Crying	
Facial expression	Smiling or inexpressive	Sad, Frightened, Frown	Rigid, Fists clenched, Knees pulled up. Pulling or pushing away. Striking out.	
Body language	Relaxed	Tense, Distressed pacing, Fidgeting	Unable to console, distract or reassure.	
Console	No need to console	Distracted or reassured by voice or touch	Unable to console, distract or reassure	
Source: * Warden, Hurley, Volicer, JAMDA 2003; 4(1): 9-15				**Total

Anxiety

The literature review for anxiety measures revealed several instruments which were valid and reliable for measuring anxiety (not prognosis), but which appeared too complicated for the end of life (EOL) population and use by multiple disciplines. These instruments included the Hamilton Anxiety Rating Scale (Hamilton, 1960), Edmonton Symptom Assessment Scale (ESAS)

(Bruera, 1991, Chang, 2000, Richardson, 2009), and the Depression Anxiety Stress Scale (DASS) (Lovibond and Lovibond, 1995; Ng, Trauer, Dodd, Callaly, Campbell and Berk, 2007).

As a result, ABC decided to create an instrument identifying the EOL symptom level of anxiety so the practitioner could implement care strategies to reduce the anxiety symptom within 4-24 hours. Anxiety-reduction interventions used at ABC, included, but were not limited to, reframing patient or caregiver perspective by the social worker; centering prayer by the spiritual care practitioner; or foot/hand massage by the nurse or home health aide. A simple four-point scale, ranging from one representing "none" to five representing "overwhelming", was created for the patient to self-rate their level of anxiety, as illustrated in Table Five.

Table 5. United Hospice of Rockland, Inc.
Anxiety Scale

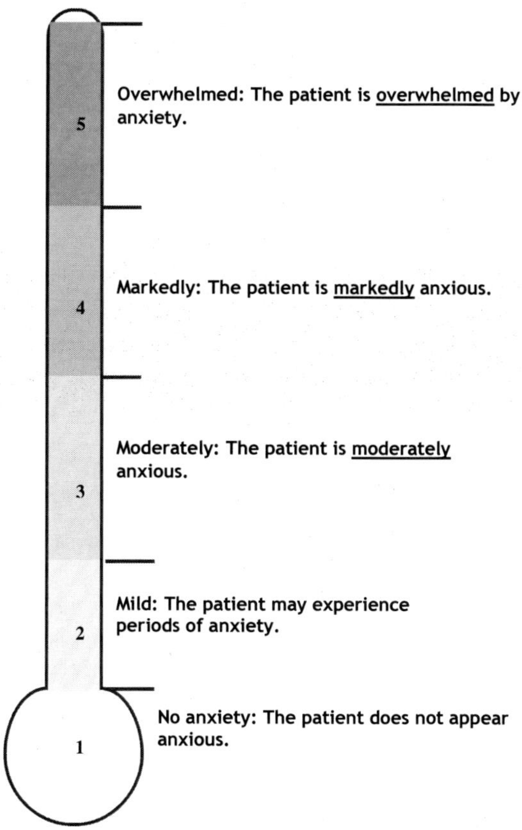

Breathing

Dyspnea, or breathlessness, is a frequent and distressing symptom experienced by most hospice patients somewhere in their trajectory of illness, regardless of their hospice diagnosis.

In searching for an operationally practical, user-friendly dyspnea instrument, the literature indicated the BORG Scale and the Modified BORG Scale (MBS) were the most commonly used, valid and reliable to measure breathlessness (Borg, 1960; Kendrick, 2003). There is extensive literature supporting the validity and reliability of both instruments, as well as their ease of use for persons experiencing shortness of breath (Ahmedzai, 2005; Bruera, 2005; LeGrand, 2002; Mahler, 1988; Mador, 1995). ABC adopted the MBS because it was the most user-friendly, evidence-based instrument, allowing staff, with patient involvement, to both identify and symptomatically treat dyspnea quickly.

The MBS is a scale rating dyspnea, using a score of 0 – 10, with "0" being no breathlessness at all and "10" meaning maximum (the worst ever) dyspnea, as illustrated in Table Six. ABC adopted a protocol to have nursing, social work and spiritual care practitioners ask the patient to rate their breathlessness during all visits. If the patient identified any level of breathlessness, the nurse is contacted for an assessment and symptom management implementation, as appropriate.

Table 6. Borg scale for dyspnea

HOW MUCH DIFFICULTY IS YOUR BREATHING NOW CAUSING YOU?

0	0.5	1	2	3	4	5	6	7	8	9	10
None	Very, very slight	Very Slight	Slight	Mod.	Somewhat Severe	Severe		Very Severe		Very, very Severe	Max

Source: Adapted from Borg, G. Psychological Bases of Perceived Exertion. *Medical Science Sports Exercise,* 1982. 14:377-381; and Kendrick, K. Baxi. S. and Smith. R. Usefulness of Modified BORG Scale in Assessing the Degree of Dyspnea in Patients with COPD and Asthma, 2004. Retrieved July 10, 2008 from www.ac6v.com/Karlaz2.htm.

IMPLEMENTATION PROCESS

The implementation plan began in July 2008 with formatting the instruments and incorporating the measurements from all six instruments into the electronic medical record for every discipline. All clinical staff received a laminated hard copy of the instruments in a convenient reference format and the staff was required to attend a mandatory educational program on the use of the tool. ABC decided to incorporate the use of the instruments into the documentation requirements for nurses, social workers and spiritual care staff. Clinical management staff was available as resources to manage the process and to support staff.

PROGRAM EVALUATION

There has not been a formal evaluation of the program. Nevertheless, staff interviews, QAPI data, and audited case reviews indicate the program has been a success. Interviews indicate staff believes the multi-instrument program has helped streamline their documentation, enhance interdisciplinary collaboration both between and during team meetings, and provided assistance with an easy, reliable means of measurement of eligibility and decline in their patients. They found the numerical rating scales valuable in their communications with other clinicians because it standardized the criteria used in assessing patients, improved tracking of progress (or lack thereof), increased the substantive basis of care planning, and facilitated interdisciplinary communication.

ABC QAPI performance improvement is a direct result of the new compliance program. The QAPI section of the new CoPs (42 CFR 418.58) requires hospices to develop, implement, and maintain an effective, ongoing, hospice-wide data driven quality assessment and performance improvement program (NHPCO, 2008b).

A comparison of ABC's medical record audit data from the last six months of 2007 to the same period in 2008 found significant improvements. For example, there was: a 25-30% improvement in the existence, specificity and completeness of documentation; a 10% improvement in the number of cases with IDT documentation recorded within 15 days; and a 40-45% increase in cases with documented compliance with LCD eligibility requirements. In addition, UHR's compliance with the "comfort within 24 hours of admission" NHPCO standards improved from 85% to above 96%.

The NHPCO standards are a set of nationally benchmarked standards designated as Primary End Results Outcome Measures (EROM) (NHPCO. 2008c). The national benchmark for the pain comfort standard is above 90%.

Since the plan inception, ABC has experienced a Medicare focused review audit. The six new instruments significantly improved documentation in patient records, particularly on patient decline on key LCD criteria. Below are two patient examples from the audit that demonstrate documentation of eligibility and hospice appropriateness, as required by specific LCDs. Both of these examples were initially denied, but subsequently reversed by NGS at the re-determination level.

Case #1: This was the case of a 97-year-old female with the hospice primary diagnosis of End Stage Heart Disease, admitted to UHR in April 2008 and dying 9 months later in January 2009. The patient was admitted to hospice care at home wanting only comfort care after discharge from a short, unsuccessful rehabilitation stay in a skilled nursing facility (SNF). The initial nursing assessment findings included: symptoms increased with activity; inability to carry on any physical activity or self-care measures; intermittently dependent on oxygen; having been optimally treated for heart disease; and not a candidate for surgical procedures. UHR's assessment was that the patient qualified for hospice services upon admission and at each recertification.

Case # 2: This was the case of an 80-year-old male with a hospice primary diagnosis of dementia, with co-morbidities of prostate cancer, chronic obstructive pulmonary disease (COPD), and hypertension. The patient was admitted to UHR in August 2008 and died in January 2009.

CONCLUSION

The ABC experience presents several lessons. First is that a hospice can simultaneously comply with regulatory requirements, reduce their audit and claim processing denial vulnerability, and improve patient QOL. Second is that hospices are well-advised to use a systematic team-based approach to problem-solving, such as a logic model, and research techniques to identify the most valid, reliable, and practical instruments to facilitate the problem-solving. Lastly, the systematic approach used in the ABC case helps inform hospices and how to select and implement measures mandated for the new quality data collection and public reporting requirements.

REFERENCES

Ahmedzai, S. and Muers, M. F. (2005). *Supportive Care in Respiratory Disease.* Chapter 8, Assessment of Dyspnea in Clinical Practice. In E. Bruera and C. M. Neumann (2005) (pages 135-143). New York: Oxford Press.

Alzheimer's Association. (2009). *2009 Alzheimer's disease Facts and Figures,* 10. Center for Disease Control National Vital Statistics Report (2008). *Deaths: Preliminary Data for 2006,* 56 (16). Chicago: Alzheimer's Association.

Anderson, F., Downing, G.M., and Hill, J. (1996). Palliative Performance Scale: A new tool. *Journal of Palliative Medicine. 12*(1); 5-11.

Arkansas Foundation of Medical Care (2005). AFMC Dyspnea Assessment Pocket Guide.indd. Retrieved May 1, 2008, from: http://www.afmc.org /quality

Borg, G. (1982). Psychophysical bases of perceived exertion. *Medical Science Sports Exercise,* 14:377-381.

Bruera, E., Keuhn, N., Miller, M.J., Selmser, and P., Macmillan, K. (1991). The Edmonton Symptom Assessment Scale (ESAS): A simple method of the assessment of palliative care patients. *Journal of Palliative Care. 7*: 6-9.

Caritas Health Group. Guidelines for using the Edmonton Symptom Assessment System (ESAS). March 2001. Retrieved June 12, 2008, from: www.palliative.org/ PC/ClinicalInfo/AssessmentTools/esas.pdf.

Chang, V. T. Hwang, S. S., and Feuerman, M. (2000). Validation of the Edmonton Symptom Assessment Scale. *Cancer. 88* (9): 2146-71.

Doberman, D., Yasar, S., and Durso, S. (2007). Would you refer this patient to hospice? An evaluation of tools for determining life expectancy in end-stage dementia. *Journal of Palliative Medicine, 10* (6), 1410- 1419.

Feldt, K.S. (2000). The checklist of non verbal pain indicators (CNPI). *Pain Management Nursing, 1*(1); 13-21.

Foley, K., Back. A., Bruera, E., et al. (2005). When the focus is on care. *Palliative Care and Cancer.* 176.

Hamilton Anxiety Rating Scale (HAM-A). Retrieved July 9, 2008, from: www.sommeil-mg.net/spip/questionaires/HAM_A.pdf.

Hamilton, M. (1960). A rating scale for depression. *Journal of Neurology, Neurosurgery and Psychiatry,* 23: 56-62.

Hanrahan, P., Raymond, M., McGowan, E., and Luchins, D. (1999), Criteria for enrolling dementia patients in hospice: a replication. *The American Journal of Hospice and Palliative Care,* 395-400.

Herr, K., Bioro, K., Decker, S. (2006). Tools for assessment of pain in non-verbal older adults with dementia. *Journal of Pain Symptom Management. 31*(2): *170-92.*

Herr, K. and Garand, L. (2001). Assessment and measurement of pain in older adults. *Clinics in Geriatric Medicine. 17*, 457-78.

Horgas, A and Miller, L. (2008), Pain assessment in people with dementia. *American Journal of Nursing, 108* (7); 62-71.

Hospice Association of America (2008). *Hospice Facts and Statistics.* Washington, DC: Hospice Association of America.

Hospice Care Conditions of Participation (2008). *Federal Register,* June 5, 2008, 42 CFR 418.1 – 418.405. Washington, DC: U. S. Government Printing Office.

Kendrick, K. R., Baxi, S., and Smith, R. M. (2004) Usefulness of the modified 0-10 Borg scale in assessing the degree of dyspnea patient with COPD and Asthma. Retrieved July 10, 2008, from: www.ac6v.com/karlaz2.htm

Karnofsky, D. A. (1948). The use of nitrogen mustards in the palliative treatment of carcinoma: With particular reference to bronchogenic carcinoma. *Cancer. 1*(4):634-56.

Lang, C., Erickson, A., Blockberger-Miller, S. and Schwien, T., (2008) Predictive modeling to improve outcomes in patients and home care. *OCS, Inc.*:1-6.

LeGrand, T. S., and Shelledy, D. C. (2002). University of Texas Health Science Center San Antonio TX: Do Asthma Symptom Scores Assigned by Respiratory Therapists Correlate with BORG Dyspnea Scores in Moderate to Severe Asthma? Retrieved July 9, 2008, from: www.cardinal.com/mps/focus/ab202/OF-02-087.asp

Lovibone, P. F. and Lovibond, S. H. (1995). The structure of negative emotional states: comparison of the Depression Anxiety Stress Scales (DASS) with Beck Depression and Anxiety Inventories. *Behavior Research and Therapy. 33:* 335-343.

Luchins, D., Hanrahan, P., and Murphy, K. (1997). Criteria for enrolling dementia patients in hospice. *Journal of the American Geriatric Association, 45* (9): 1054-1059.

Lynn, J. (2004). *Sick to death and not going to take it anymore!: Reforming health care for the last years of life.* Berkeley, CA: University of California Press.

Mahler, D. and Wells, C. (1988). Evaluation of clinical methods for rating Dyspnea. *Chest, 93*:580-586.

Mador, M.J., Rodis, A, and Magalang, U. J. (1995). Reproducibility of Borg Scale Measurements of Dyspnea during Exercise in Patients with COPD. *Chest, 107*:1590-1597.

McCafferty, M. and Pasero, C. (2d Ed.) (1999) *Pain: A Clinical Manual.* Mosby, Inc.

Medicare Payment Advisory Commission (2012). Report to the Congress: Medicare Payment Policy. Chapter 11, March 2012. Washington, DC: MedPac.

Mitchell, S., Kiely, D., Hamel, M., Park, P., Morris, J. and Fries, B. (2004). Estimating prognosis for nursing home residents with advanced dementia. *Journal of the American Medical Association, 291* (22):2734-2740.

Morita, T., Tsunoda, J., Inoue, S. et al. (1999). Validity of the Palliative Performance Scale from a survival perspective. *Journal of Pain and Symptom Management, 18*(2):2-3.

Morita, T., Tsunoda, J., Inoue, S., Chihara, S. (2000). Survival prediction of terminally ill cancer patients by clinical symptoms: Development of a simple indicator. *Clinical Oncology. 29*(3):156-159.

Moses, S. (2009) Everyday Health (2008). Family Practice Notebook, LLC. 2008. Retrieved March 30, 2009, from: www.Fpnotebook.com /Psych/Exam/HmltnAnxtyScl.htm

Murdock, J. and Larien, D. (2004). Assessing pain in cognitively impaired older adults. *Nursing Standards. 18* (38): 33-39.

National Hospice and Palliative Care Organization (2009a). *Hospice Care in America: NHPCO Facts and Figures on Hospice Care*. Alexandria, VA: National Hospice and Palliative Care Organization.

National Hospice and Palliative Care Organization (2009b). Retrieve May 24, 2009, from: http://www.nhpco.org/i4a/pages/index.cfm?pageid=5624

National Hospice and Palliative Care Organization (2009c). *End Results Outcome Measure results.* Retrieved May 24, 2009, from: http://www.nhpco.org/i4a/pages/ Index.cfm?pageID=4765

National Hospice and Palliative Care Organization (2011). CMS Proposed Rule for Hospice Quality Reporting. Alexandria, VA: NHPCO.

National Hospice and Palliative Care Organization (2012). NHPCO Facts and Figures: Hospice Care in America. Alexandria, VA: NHPCO.

Nekolaichuk, C., Watanabe, S., and Beaumont, C. (2008). The Edmonton Symptom Assessment System: A 15 year retrospective review of validation studies (1991-2006). *Palliative Medicine, 22* (2):111-22.

Ng, F., Trauer, T, Dodd, S., Callaly, T., Campbell, S., and Berk, M., (2007). The validity of the 21-item version of the Depression Anxiety Stress Scale as a routine clinical outcome measure. *Acta Neuropsychiatrica. 19*:304-310.

Olson, K. Turner, R. Courneya, K. Field, C.Godfrey, M., Cree, M., and Hanson, J. (2008). Possible links between behavioral and physiological indices of tiredness, fatigue, and exhaustion in advanced cancer. *Supportive Care in Cancer. 16* (3): 241-249.

Pratt, M. (2012). Hospice Quality reporting Program. Power-point presentation for the National Association for Home Care and Hospice, March 26, 2012. Washington, D. C.

Pujpl, L., Katz, N., and Zacharoff, J. (2007). PainEDU.Manual: A Pocket Guide to Pain Management. Inflexion, Inc. Retrieved June 15, 2008, from: www.PainEDU.org

Richardson, L.A. (2009). A review of the reliability and validity of the Edmonton Symptom Management System. *Current Oncology, 16* (1)*:* 55.

Reisberg, B. (1988). Functional assessment staging (FAST). *Psychopharmacology Bulletin, 24* (4): 653-659.

Ross, C. (2010. QAPI: How do you measure up? Preparing for public reporting in hospice: An overview for success. *Home Healthcare Nurse 29*(1): 45-51.

Schonwetter, R., Han, B., Small, B., Marin, B., Tope, K. and Haley, W. (2003) Predictors of six-month survival among patients with dementia: an evaluation of hospice Medicare guidelines. *American Journal of Hospice and Palliative Care, 20* (2): 105-11

The Corridor Group (2008). Hospice Quickflips: The Corridor Guide for Hospice Clinicians, National Government Services Version. The Corridor Group.

Virik, K. and Glare, P. (2002). Validation of the Palliative Performance Scale for inpatients admitted to a palliative care unit in Sydney, Australia. *Journal of Pain and Symptom Management. 23*(6): 455-7.

Warden, V., Hurley, A., and Volicer, L. (2003). Development and psychometric evaluation of the Pain Assessment in Advanced Dementia (PAINAD) Scale. *Journal American Medical Directors Association,* 4: 9-15.

Ware, L., Epps, C., Herr, K., and Packard, A., Evaluation of the revised faces pain scale, verbal descriptor scale, numeric rating scale, and Iowa pain thermometer in older minority adults. *Pain Management Nursing.* Retrieved June 12, 2008, from www.medscape.com.

Weatherbee Resources, Inc. (2008). *CoPs in a Book: The Final Edition.* Hyannis, MA. Weatherbee Resources, Inc.

Wilner, F.S., and Arnold, R. (2004). The Palliative Performance Scale. Fast Facts and concepts #125. End of Life Palliative Education Resource Center. Retrieved June 12, 2009, from: www.eperc.mcw.edu

Wong-Baker. F. A. (2005).CES Pain Rating Scale. In Hockenberry, M. J., Wilson D., and Winkelstein, M. L. (Eds.) (7th Ed.) (2005) (page 1259). *Wong's Essentials of Pediatric Nursing*. St Louis: Mosby.

In: Hospice Care
Editors: J. Hanl and S. Koeck

ISBN: 978-1-62618-456-5

Chapter 5

Implementation of Hospice and Palliative Medicine Training in the United States to Meet Patients' End-of-Life Needs

Thomas Bui

Kaiser Permanente Hospice and Palliative Medicine
Fellowship Training Program, Portland, OR, US

Abstract

Effectively training palliative care professionals has direct benefits to the critically ill patients and reduces the end-of-life distress for these patients' families. Adaptations within the Accreditation Council of Graduate Medical Education (ACGME) uphold resident physicians' formal training in palliative medicine and end-of-life symptom management.

Such changes are preparing a critical mass of physicians in the United States to competently address seriously ill and dying patients' medical, emotional, and spiritual needs. Healthcare policy options dovetail with palliative medical education steadily at multiple levels of medical training—namely, medical school curriculum mandates, requiring residency training programs to foster patient-centered communication skills and discussions about advanced directives, and instituting palliative medicine proficiency Continuing Medical Education (CME) requirements for all states' medical licensing boards. Healthcare reform proposals must also evolve to redefine the National Health Service Corps (NHSC) post-graduate training over the next five years and the Hospice Medicare Benefit altogether. Clinical research in end of life care and leveraging Internet-based didactic technologies increase physicians' access to excellence in the field of hospice and palliative medicine. Correcting our current paucity of formal training in palliative medicine in the United States is a realistic goal and restores patients' dignity at the end of life.

Background

Many people in the United States die without dignity due to the widening gap between the need for palliative care services and the supply of trained palliative care professionals.

Hospice is the end-of-life medical setting in which palliative medicine specialists competently address seriously ill and dying patients' medical, emotional, and spiritual needs. Without formal training in palliative medicine and end-of-life pain management, physicians in the United States are less equipped to provide their patients the necessary pain relief modalities and their patients' family resources. Furthermore, an incorrect association of hospice with physician-assisted suicide or with forgoing potentially life-prolonging treatments precludes patients' access to end-of-life palliation. Avoidance of death in the terminally ill is part of the current and urgent problem of a broken end-of-life policy in the United States.

The paucity of formal training in palliative medicine thus under-utilizes hospice, the most comprehensive program to provide palliative health care in the United States. President Obama signed comprehensive health reform into law in March 2010 with the goal of implementing health care workforce changes by 2011.

The proposed time line called for an establishment of Teaching Health Centers to provide payments for primary care residency programs in community-based ambulatory patient care centers. At present, the Accreditation Council for Graduate Medical Education (ACGME) administers residency training not only for primary care but also for subspecialty training, such as Palliative Medicine.

However, only 25% of hospitals and 70% of academic medical centers offered inpatient palliative care consultation. Reflective of systemic under-utilization and lack of appropriate referral patterns, only 30% of patients are enrolled in hospice at the time of death.

Problem

Terminally ill patients do not currently die with dignity in the United States due to lack of training on the part of health care professionals. Health care reform as of early 2013 has not adequately addressed the fact that the United States graduate medical education system must adopt a preferred alternative or educating primary care providers to proficiently counsel patients on end-of-life care. Requiring all patients' involvement in the palliative medicine process is equally important; mandatory completion of a Physician Orders for Life-Sustaining Treatment (POLST) form when getting driver's license ensures that patients communicate in written form their end-of-life decision preferences. The problem is avoidance of death, which intuitively is unavoidable, rather than focusing on quality and quantity of life.

In American culture, discussion of death is not a popular topic. Thus, debate about how to best allocate resources at the end of life reflects that effort to deal with the inevitable by simply relying on progressively sophisticated technology to "buy time." In practical terms, an otherwise healthy 20-year-old swimmer, who while drowning would likely sustain rib fractures with the appropriate chest compressions of cardiopulmonary resuscitation (CPR), and yet her respiratory recovery may be confounded more by the delayed healing of her fractured ribs than the drowning itself. All too frequently, health care professionals find themselves ill-equipped to address time-sensitive decisions to perform CPR on physiologically compromised 85-year-old patients.

Lack of preparation is then coupled with failure to communicate health care decision-making proxies in advance. Next, panic on the part of well-meaning family members nonetheless compels health care professionals to buy time by performing CPR on all comers. This practice unfortunately relegates very sick young and old patients to ventilator dependence from which they have a difficult time recovering from.

As a result, terminally ill patients do not currently die with dignity in the United States. Lack of training on the part of health care professionals to address the Palliative Medicine needs of terminally ill patients is part of the problem. Physicians must be more proficient at the management of the imminently dying patient. This education must include care of medical disorders, effective communication, and coordination with the medical care team.

Other part of the problem is that as a nation, we have not articulated a plan to empower patients to consider what care plan they would like implemented when they are deemed terminal. Decision making of patients must be grounded in the principles of hospice and palliative medicine, ethics, and appropriate law. Interdisciplinary care planning optimizes the use of hospice, and systems of palliative care can thus better serve populations with advanced illness.

POLICY OPTIONS

Medical School Curriculum Mandates

Medical school education must provide physician students training with prognostic tools. Medical students must learn to enhance quality of life that should be offered alongside curative and/or restorative medical care in all medical settings. When implemented as a medical school curriculum policy, teaching medical students appropriate triage for the inclusion of more patients with advanced stages of non-cancer diagnoses (such as heart failure, chronic obstructive pulmonary disease, and dementia) in specialized hospice programs would improve quality of life in those terminal patients.

The American College of Cardiology (ACC) itself has tried to improve the use of the New York Heart Association Classification of Congestive Heart Failure by medical trainees using objective metrics rather than subjective functional measures. Neither method is perfect and can be discordant to correctly predict time till death. In the United States, Medicare pays for hospice care; so correct prognostication is vital to determine who pays for what. Early on in their medical school training, physicians must thus understand the economic, public policy, and clinical implications of hospice care. Research such as that produced by the ACC will help physicians-in-training understand that treatment in hospice care might allow more patients to die with optimal medical care in the advanced stages of their illnesses. Mandating hospice care education into medical school curricula empowers medical students to consider palliative care a key component of excellent medical care, not an alternative to be pursued only after other approaches have been exhausted.

The ACGME Residency Requirements

The Accreditation Council for Graduate Medical Education (ACGME) is a private, non-profit council that evaluates and accredits more than 9,000 residency programs across 135 specialties and subspecialties in the United States. The ACGME is charged with regulating all US graduate physician residency training, including scholarships. What would an ACGME-accredited training program emphasizing Palliative Medicine look like? It must establish mechanisms to foster excellence in the specialty field of hospice and palliative medicine consistent with the competency initiative launched by the ACGME in 2002 called the Outcome Project.

As a result of this project, ACGME identified 6 ACGME Core Competencies to be used by programs to evaluate their residents in training. Training programs must define the specific knowledge, skills, behaviors, and attitudes required, and provide educational experiences as needed in order for their residents to practice in their respective fields. In September 2006, ABMS approved the creation of Hospice and Palliative Medicine (HPM) as a sub-specialty; a 12-month ACGME-accredited fellowship program is required for trainees after 2012. How would such a fellowship program incorporate the ACGME Core Competencies? An example is as follows:

1. *PATIENT CARE:*
   The resident should demonstrate sound clinical judgment about therapeutic interventions based on patient information and preferences, existing scientific evidence, and compassionate, appropriate, and effective care in collaboration with an interdisciplinary team. Residents will work with health care professionals, including those from other disciplines, to provide patient-focused care, aimed at maximizing well-being and quality of life for patients with advanced, progressive, life-threatening illnesses and their families.
2. *MEDICAL KNOWLEDGE:*
   The resident should know the basic and clinically supportive sciences which are relevant to the care of patients with life-threatening illnesses and to their families and apply this knowledge to hospice and palliative care practice. Residents will investigate and critically analyze knowledge about established and evolving biomedical, clinical, public health, population science, and social sciences.
3. *PRACTICE-BASED LEARNING AND IMPROVEMENT:*
   The resident should be able to systematically investigate, evaluate, and improve their practices in caring for patients and families by performing practice-based improvement activities. In the investigation and evaluation of care for their own population of patients, residents

will appraise and assimilate scientific evidence relevant to palliative care to improve patient care for the larger population from which their patients are drawn.

4. *INTERPERSONAL AND COMMUNICATION SKILLS:*
   The resident should develop therapeutic and ethically sound interpersonal relationships with patients and build strong communication skills, especially about end-of-life discussions, with patients, their families, and professional associates. Residents will collaborate on healthcare teams implementing effective listening skills to elicit and provide information using effective nonverbal, explanatory, questioning, and writing skills. Residents will develop patient-centered processes for medical decision making that result from effective relationship-building, exchanging information, and emotional support.
5. *PROFESSIONALISM:*
   The resident should demonstrate sensitivity and responsiveness to fellow healthcare professionals' as well as patients' diverse culture, age, gender, and disabilities. Residents' responsiveness to the needs of patients and society shall supersede self-interest; adhere to ethical principles; as well as enhance quality of life and reduce suffering. Ongoing professional development and appropriate self-reflection exhibit residents' accountability to patients, society and their profession.
6. *SYSTEMS BASED PRACTICE:*
   The resident should be able to partner with internal health care managers and external healthcare agencies to assess, coordinate, and improve health care and know how these activities can provide their patients high-quality care. Residents will be able effectively call on system resources and other community-based resources for patients to affect overall health system performance for patients and their families. Particular for their hospice and palliative patient population, residents' responsiveness to the larger context will significantly help patients' families navigate system of health care during a challenging time in their lives.

As a good way to attract qualified physicians to the palliative medicine field, medical school loan repayment programs would allow ACGME resident physicians to advance the palliative medicine discipline. The Steven Thompson Loan Repayment Program (STLRP) administered by the Medical

Board of California is a model program, whereby primary care physicians practicing in medically underserved areas have their medical school loans up to US$105,000 forgiven by the State of California. The STLRP template, in fact, requires 15% of recipients to practice in a geriatric setting; so, this would be an easy model for the ACGME to adopt as a policy for palliative physicians' medical school loan forgiveness.

This ACGME physician residency education policy would also specifically address the shortage of palliative and hospice physicians in California. In California, only 4 Palliative Medicine fellowship training programs exist. The ACGME should also collaborate with the American Academy of Hospice and Palliative Medicine (AAHPM), which recognizes the shortage of palliative physicians and has thus implemented a plan, which was to ''grandfather'' physicians to palliative medicine specialty certification. This educational process encourages those physicians trained through the ACGME to become certified after they had more than 400 hours of taking care of terminally ill patients. The ACGME must now determine whether and how to extend the grandfathering period past 2012.

Even as the ACGME weighs in, several medical centers acknowledge that, due to the current shortage of Palliative Medicine fellowship-trained physicians, these palliative medicine jobs will be given even without the fellowship training.

To have uniform palliative care and hospice standards and to train greater number of clinicians to close the substantial gap between need and availability, the AAHPM supports public and private funding mechanisms to ensure the growth and development of ACGME certified palliative medicine fellowship programs. Such programs are essential. Processes of these envisioned ACGME graduate medical education programs specifically designate a set of specialist-level skills and practices which must be offered by credentialed specialists in hospice and palliative medicine.

Continuing Medical Education Requirements for State Licensure

Continuing medical education requirements are routine for all states' medical licensing boards and are a viable method to regulate palliative medical education proficiency. With the field of palliative medicine evolving, physicians must be kept abreast of medical advances in the specialty and their terminal patients' care. The American Medical Association (AMA) Council on

Ethical and Judicial Affairs in November 2010 encouraged physicians to participate in their patients' advance care planning, including Durable Power of Attorney for Health care. This medico-legal policy stance was influenced to some degree on defensively practiced medicine rather than doing what is best for the patient but nonetheless proactively required end-of-life care discussions.

Recently, the American Thoracic Society also recommended that the AMA encourage the Centers for Medicare and Medicaid Services to designate voluntary discussions about end-of-life care. Physicians will be required to submit proof of completion of courses on medical care in the palliative set-ting as covered services in the 2012 Medicare Physician Fee Schedule. In addition, they will be better equipped to question use of public funds and hold policymakers to task in the creation of health care budgets.

SUPPORTING ARGUMENT

As a physician myself, I support palliative medicine education at the medical school stage because this philosophical stance needs to be inculcated early in physician training.

Medical school curriculums afford most of the time of medical professionals with relatively fewer clinical responsibilities and waiting until residency training to learn these concepts is too late. Researchers have shown that structured didactic and experiential palliative care during the clinical clerkships of medical student education manifests as significant and largely sustained improvements in end-of-life discussions compared to a national sample of residents and attending physicians.

In fact, some graduate ACGME medical specialties, such as Radiology, have very little direct patient contact so it does not make sense to wait till that ACGME residency training phase. On the other hand, Oncologists who are very attuned to the death process must be trained early on. The palliative medicine consultants indeed act as an extension of the oncology care team so the oncologists can focus on giving chemotherapy treatments. At the same time, all medical doctors must realize that dealing with death and dying are part of the medical praxis.

Many patients are not aware of the Hospice Medicare Benefit and rely on their physician to guide them in the emotionally taxing time of end of life. Hospice Medicare Benefit and other end-of-life topics fit well into the ethics components curricula of many medical schools. Medical school curricula should emphasize the humanistic approach, so that physicians can care for their patients comprehensively, including knowledgeable advocacy at the time around death.

OPPOSING ARGUMENT

Requiring palliative medicine training in the medical school curriculum is unrealistic and logistically untenable. Basic science classes are meant to focus on fundamental anatomy, and pathophysiology principles are already overwhelmed with the sheer volume of material requiring mastery. In addition, at the medical school pre-clinical stage, the medical students have fewer interactions with patients so these philosophical issues have less relevance. It is more reasonable to inform the public about hospice and have consumer-driven demand for palliative medicine in life-limiting illnesses. Continued experimentation with the curriculum for problem-based learning has arguably not produced better doctors.

Under the current practice of residency training for post-graduate studies in the United States, Medicare pays for ACGME training. To envision a new teaching health center program does address the lack of primary care physicians in the United States with palliative medicine specialty training, but it overlooks the fundamental ongoing problem of geographical misdistribution of such health care providers.

Furthermore, the legislated timeline proposed by Obama was inaccurate to start with because training programs recruit medical school graduates over a year in advance through an annual complex application–interview cycle called ''The Match.'' Therefore, it would not have been practical to implement the proposed changes until 2012 at which point the new centers would also not likely be in place functionally yet.

President Obama's health care reform law is supposed to somehow raise $1.5 billion for the National Health Service Corps postgraduate training over 5 years, which would actually delay palliative medicine training. Medical education incorporating end-of-life training can instead be part of medical licensure from the start. Respecting life requires discussion of end-of-life decisions in the medical school curriculum, which is relatively relaxed setting of non-acute medical care. Waiting to address these issues under times of physical and emotional duress of a medical emergency in the intensive care unit setting is a recipe for misunderstanding and defensive practice of medicine.

Recommendation for Action

The United States health care system serves its citizens most effectively during end-of-life care by training physicians in hospice care. The clinical evidence on quality of patient care strongly recommends early implementation of palliative medicine training in physicians' skills sets. One of the strongest reasons to incorporate palliative medicine in to the medical school curriculum is that it is cost effective. Palliative care consultations not only reduce costs but also improve quality of the remaining life for the sickest (i.e., most expensive) patients that physicians provide health care for. The early inculcating of a philosophical stance that life itself and quality of life are sacred is another reason palliative medicine principles must be required in the medical school curriculum.

Requiring all patients' involvement in the palliative medicine process is equally important; mandatory completion of a POLST form when getting driver's license ensures that patients communicate in a written form about their end-of-life decision preferences. Similarly, the collaborative physician–patient covenant aligns an individual patient's palliative care wishes with their tailored treatments; this also ensures that patients and their families are comfortable and supported in the end-of-life health care phase.

The routine integrating of end-of-life discussions into primary care physician visits removes the stigma of palliative medicine as a "giving up" of care. Instead, patients are given advance notice that palliative care can help with their eventual end-of-life symptom management and concomitant psychosocial support so that patients can continue treatments. In turn, hospice programs staffed by a critical mass of physicians specializing in palliative medicine can provide a greater number of patients palliative care support before they qualify for hospice. Patients involved in this process will have working fluency to request hospice care sooner and maximize their cost-effective Medicare Hospice Benefit for longer lengths of stay.

Physicians trained early on in their medical education about the patient's health advantages with hospice, including reduced hospital re-admissions. These changes thus end up saving the US health care system literally thousands of dollars per hospitalized patient. Loan forgiveness programs for physicians working in palliative medicine, similar to the STLRP template in California, are a feasible method to attract the best physicians to the palliative medicine field.

In conclusion, early implementation of palliative medicine training in physicians' skills sets during medical school curricula is solidly based on clinical evidence regarding quality of patient care. Such training by hospice programs shall yield a critical mass of physicians specializing in palliative medicine. Only in this way can health care in the United States provide a greater number of patients palliative care support before they qualify for hospice and ultimately be the cost-effective way for Americans to enjoy quality of life as well as quality of dying.

REFERENCES

[1] Field MJ, Behrman RE, Committee on Palliative and End-of-Life Care for Children and Their Families. *When Children Die: Improving Palliative and End-of-Life Care for Children and Their Families.* Washington, DC: The National Academies Press; 2003.

[2] Head BA, Earnshaw LA, Greenberg RB, Morehead RC, Pfeifer MP, Shaw MA."I will never forget": what we learned from medical student reflections on a palliative care experience. *J. Palliat. Med.* 2012 May; 15(5):535-41.

[3] Morrison LJ, Thompson BM, Gill AC. A required third-year medical student palliative care curriculum impacts knowledge and attitudes. *J. Palliat. Med.* 2012 Jul;15(7):784-9.

[4] Morrison RS, Meier DE. Clinical practice. Palliative care. *N. Eng. J. Med.* 2004; 350(25): 2582-2590.

[5] Nelson C, Chand P, Sortais J, Oloimooja J, Rembert G. Inpatient palliative care consults and the probability of hospital readmission. *Perm. J.* 2011; 15(2): 48-51.

[6] Gazelle G. Understanding hospice–an underutilized option for life's final chapter. *N. Eng. J. Med.* 2007; 357(4): 321-324.

[7] Quill TE. Perspectives on care at the close of life. Initiating end-of-life discussions with seriously ill patients: addressing the ''elephant in the room''. *JAMA*. 2000; 284(19): 2502-2507.

[8] Seoane L, Bourgeois DA, Blais CM, Rome RB, Luminais HH, Taylor DE. Teaching palliative care in the intensive care unit: how to break the news. *Ochsner. J.* 2012 Winter;12(4):312-7.

[9] von Gunten CF, Mullan P, Nelesen RA, Soskins M, Savoia M, Buckholz G, Weissman DE. Development and evaluation of a palliative medicine curriculum for third-year medical students. *J. Palliat. Med.* 2012 Nov;15(11):1198-217.

[10] Wright AA, Katz IT. Letting go of the rope–aggressive treatment, hospice care and open access. *N. Eng. J. Med.* 2007; 357(4): 324-327.

In: Hospice Care
Editors: J. Hanl and S. Koeck

ISBN: 978-1-62618-456-5

Chapter 6

BRIDGING THE GAP IN END-OF-LIFE CARE DECISION MAKING

***Alaina J. Brown*[1] *and Teresa P. Díaz-Montes*[2*]**

[1] Division of Gynecologic Oncology, The University of Texas MD Anderson Cancer Center, Houston, TX, US

[2] Division of Gynecologic Oncology, Department of Obstetrics and Gynecology, The Johns Hopkins Medical Institutions, Baltimore, MD, US

ABSTRACT

End-of-life care (EOLC) decision-making plays a prominent role in the field of Gynecologic Oncology. Gynecologic oncologists are unique among surgical oncologists because they often become their patient's primary provider and are responsible for the patient's surgical and medical management. As a result, a close bond forms between the physician and the patient. The gynecologic oncologist is oftentimes the provider responsible for initiating EOLC conversations and making EOLC decisions with terminally ill patients. EOLC planning allows the patient to easily transition from the active treatment of cancer to the management of the physical, spiritual, and emotional needs of the dying patient. Without clear and frank discussions regarding patient preferences

* Corresponding author: Teresa P. Díaz-Montes, MD, MPH, Division of Gynecologic Oncology, Johns Hopkins Medical Institutions, 600 North Wolfe Street / Phipps 281, Baltimore, MD 21287. Phone: 410-955-8240; Fax: 410-614-8718; e-mail: tdiazmo1@jhmi.edu.

for EOLC, the patient's voice may get lost. Previous research has examined the importance of communication regarding EOLC preferences and has begun to lay the groundwork for effective dialogue between physicians and gynecologic oncology patients on this delicate topic. The main objective of this review is to evaluate the factors that play a role in the integration of EOLC into clinical practice.

INTRODUCTION

End-of-life care (EOLC) decision-making plays a prominent role in the field of Gynecologic Oncology. An estimated 88,750 women in the United States will be diagnosed with a gynecologic malignancy and 29,520 will die during 2012 from their disease [1]. Gynecologic Oncologists are unique among surgical oncologists because they oftentimes become their patient's primary provider and are responsible for the patient's surgical and medical management. As a result, a close bond forms between the physician and the patient. The gynecologic oncologist oftentimes is the provider responsible for making EOLC decisions with terminal patients.

EOLC planning is important to allow the patient to easily transition from active treatment of cancer to management of the physical, spiritual, and emotional needs of the dying patient. Without clear and frank discussions regarding patient preferences for EOLC, the patient's voice may get lost. When seriously ill patients are near the end of life, they and their families find it difficult to decide what the best course of action is. In, these instances, patients rely on their physicians or other trusted health care agents for guidance. In the best of circumstances, the patient, the family and the physician have held discussions about treatment options, chance of success, overall prognosis, and the patients' quality of life during and after the treatment. Ideally, these discussions should continue as the patients' condition change. Physicians must have an understanding of the patient's desires in terms EOLC documentation such as Do Not Resuscitate/Do Not Intubate (DNR/DNI) orders and Advanced Directives as well as general preferences regarding Hospice care. Frequently such discussions are not held. In the event that the patient becomes incapacitated to make decisions, the family and the physician are forced to make decisions based on what they think the patient would want creating a lot of stress. The main objective of this review is to evaluate the factors that play a role in the integration of EOLC discussions into clinical practice.

THE IMPORTANCE OF END-OF-LIFE CARE DISCUSSIONS

Although difficult, EOLC discussions are an important component to provide comprehensive and quality oncologic care at the end-of-life. The National Comprehensive Cancer Network recommends that EOLC discussions should be held between providers and terminally ill cancer patients who have a life expectancy of less than one year [2]. Early, frank discussions regarding EOLC preferences with oncology patients provide two benefits. First, they allow the patient to express their wishes regarding the end-of-life in a controlled environment that is free of the immediate pressures of death. Second, early discussions allow for the terminally ill patient to exert control over her disease status by enabling the patient to have the final say regarding the manner in which she dies.

Despite the benefits of EOLC conversation, the number of provider-patient EOLC conversations is low. Studies indicate that only 9 - 39% of oncology patients have discussed EOLC preferences with their providers [3-5]. Patients aware of their terminal status were more likely to have had these conversations (56%) [3]. It has been pointed out that discussion rates are low due to providers hesitancy to initiate EOLC conversations due to: fear of being perceived as negative, the stress regarding making an incorrect prognosis, or the time that is consumed to adequately address the issue especially in this era of time constrains [6, 7]. However, EOLC discussions are greatly desired by patients [4, 8, 9]. The majority of patients, 58–75% , desires that their physicians initiate a conversation about advanced directives if the physician thoughts it is appropriate for the patient's disease state [9]. Patients given the opportunity to discuss EOLC preferences with their physicians are more likely to receive the care they desire at the end-of-life [3]. Additionally, patients who have discussed EOLC preferences are less likely to undergo resuscitation, intubation, or ICU admission near the end-of-life and are more likely to be referred to hospice at an earlier time [5].

End-of-life discussions may have cascading benefits for patients and their caregivers. Despite physicians concerns of increase emotional distress and psychological harm due to these discussions, not an association has been established. On the contrary, the worst outcomes are seen in patients who did not report EOL conversations. This patient population received significantly more aggressive medical care in their final week of life, which was associated with worse patient quality of life near death. In addition, their bereaved caregivers experienced worse quality of life, more regret, and were at higher risk for developing a Major Depressive Disorder a median of 6.5 months later

[5]. Patients who reported EOL discussions received less aggressive medical care and were more likely to receive hospice services for more than one week. Less aggressive care and earlier hospice referrals were associated with better patient quality of life near death. Early hospice referrals is key as patients who received less than one week of hospice care had the same quality of life scores as patients who did not receive hospice at all. Better patient quality of life near death, in turn, is associated with better quality of life among surviving caregivers who experienced less regret and showed improvements in self-reported health, physical functioning, mental health, and overall quality of life during the bereavement period.

Factors Affecting End-of-Life Care Decisions

Many factors such as age, race, time and religion may affect the patient's approach to discussing EOLC issues. Research demonstrates that elderly patients overall desire less aggressive treatment than younger patients [10-12]. Elderly patients were more likely to withhold resuscitative or life-sustaining treatment such as CPR, ventilator support, surgery or dialysis [10, 12]. Conversely, younger patients with dependent children are more likely to desire aggressive treatment to prolong life [13]. Additionally, they are more likely to defer EOLC decisions regarding DNR/DNI and other advanced directives [4, 13].

Race is another factor that oftentimes affects EOLC decision making, utilization of aggressive life sustaining measures, and hospice enrollment. Several studies demonstrate that minorities' utilization of life-prolonging EOLC measures at the end-of-life is greater than Caucasians [14-16]. African Americans and Hispanics are more likely to desire interventions such as mechanical ventilation and the administration of life-prolonging drugs that make them feel ill when compared to Caucasians who are less likely to desire these interventions [16]. This discrepancy may be due to something as simple as miscommunication between the patient and the provider. One study demonstrated that although EOLC discussions between African American patients and their providers oftentimes resulted in DNR orders, African American patients with DNR orders were no less likely to receive prolongment of the end-of-life when compared to their counterparts without DNR orders [15].

The increased utilization of life-prolonging medical measures leads to increased in-hospital deaths and decreased utilization of hospice services at the end-of-life. Among Medicare patients ages 65 and older, more African Americans (18%) and Hispanics (15%) desired to die in the hospital when compared to Caucasians (8%) [16]. Caucasians were noted to utilize hospice more frequently (26%) compared to 20% for African Americans and 23% for Hispanics [14].

End-of-life decision making requires time. Most patients need to process the idea that life is nearing its end before they can make decisions about their EOLC.

When discussions begin in the last 30 days of life, the end-of-life period is typically already under way. Importantly, clinicians may not know when the last month of life is about to begin. However, physicians seem to wait until the patient begins deteriorating medically, a strategy that leads to a high incidence of inpatient discussions. Instead, physicians should consider moving conversations closer to diagnosis and initiating conversations while the patient is doing comparatively well, so the patient has time to plan for more difficult times in the future.

Religion and spirituality (R/S) are important to patients diagnosed with cancer because they provide a way for the patient to cope with and understand their illness [17, 18]. Roberts et al. surveyed 108 women with varying stages of cancer and 38 women with benign disease found that 76% of those surveyed believed that religion had a serious place in their lives [19]. Forty-nine percent stated they had become more religious since their cancer diagnosis [19]. None of the women surveyed had become less religious since their cancer diagnosis [19]. Ninety-three percent stated that their religion helped sustain their hopes [19]. Religious coping "can offer patients a sense of meaning, comfort, control and personal growth while facing life threatening illness" [20].

R/S also provided a framework for EOLC decision making by allowing for the formation of ethical guidelines that provide "insight and normative guidance for making decisions" [21].

Accordingly, it is no surprise that an individual patient's decisions regarding EOLC planning are greatly influenced by their R/S. Individuals utilizing a high level of religious coping were more likely to receive intensive life-prolonging care near death when compared to patients with a low level of religious coping (13.6% vs. 4.2%) [20]. Additionally, these patients were more likely to receive mechanical ventilation (11.3% vs. 3.6%), undergo cardiopulmonary resuscitation (7.4% vs. 1.8%) and die in the ICU (10.7 vs. 4.2%) [20].

The Communication Gap between Physicians and Patients

Despite patients' desire to communicate EOLC preferences, oftentimes physicians are unaware of patient's desires. Hamel et al. demonstrated that physicians did not know the preferences of 25% of their patients [10]. Physician assessment of patient preferences regarding comfort care versus prolonging life was correct in 45% of patients and incorrect for 31% [10]. Another study among 32 patients with breast cancer found that 75% had collected information regarding advanced directives and 66% had already written advance directives [22]. For these 32 patients, providers knew about the advanced directive in only 14% of cases [22]. These patients reported that they were three times more likely to discuss written advanced directives with family and friends than with their providers [22].

Physicians may not feel equipped to discuss end-of-life care. The lack of physician training in this area and fear may lead to discomfort when discussing end-of-life. Physicians are foremost trained to be scientists. As scientists, physician tends to focus on curing diseases. Physicians are inhibited in communicating with the patient because they don't know what to do with the natural fears and anxieties that go with the illness. The emotional pain of patients is more frightening to deal with than the physical pain. This is especially true when the physician is the bearer of bad news. It can be very challenging to tell the patient and the family that the treatment is not working and that death is on the horizon. Delivering bad news is like admitting failure. Physicians are success-oriented and to admit failure to cure is damaging to their professional and personal self-esteem.

Bridging the Gap

As providers, we have a responsibility to understand our patients' desires for the end-of-life. It is imperative that we take the opportunity to discuss EOLC decisions with our patients before they become too ill to make educated decisions regarding their care. We need to provide them with appropriate time and space. The initiation of dialogue is oftentimes difficult and as providers, we must recognize that we are oftentimes overly optimistic regarding our patient's prognoses [23, 24]. As a result we may defer these conversations until there is little time for the patient and her family to fully explore their

EOLC decisions. Having one conversation about end-of-life is not enough to address all the issues. Ongoing discussions should be held as circumstances change and new information comes to light. While difficult, these discussions must be initiated. Appropriate strategies vary from patient to patient and require a keen understanding of the patients' motivations and goals for management of her disease. Our patients entrust us with the ability to care for them in times of illness. It is our responsibility to be cognitive of the choices they must face as they approach the end-of-life and to encourage them to engage in a dialogue regarding their desires.

CONCLUSION

Although this technique cannot correct for unmeasured or hidden biases, such as how a patients' prior experiences with death may influence their attitudes to EOL discussions or decision-making, it is one of the most robust statistical methods available to correct for potential selection bias and confounding. Nevertheless, it is possible that patients who have a preference for less aggressive medical care may be more likely to initiate EOL discussions with their physicians. Alternatively, it is possible that the timing of EOL discussions is important, or that EOL discussions are a proxy for physician factors which may determine medical treatment at the EOL (e.g., physicians who have EOL discussions may limit their patients' exposure to aggressive medical measures by choosing not to hospitalize patients with terminal illness).

REFERENCES

[1] American Cancer Society Cancer Facts and Figures 2012 [7/25/12]. Available from: http://www.cancer.org/acs/groups/content/@ epidemio logysurveilance/documents/document/acspc-031941.pdf.

[2] National Comprehensive Cancer Network: Practice Guidelines in Oncology. Available from: http://www.nccn.org/professionals/ physician_gls/f_guidelines.asp - supportive.

[3] Mack JW, Weeks JC, Wright AA, Block SD, Prigerson HG. End-of-life discussions, goal attainment, and distress at the end of life: predictors

and outcomes of receipt of care consistent with preferences. *J Clin Oncol* 2010;28(7):1203-8.

[4] Diaz-Montes TP, Johnson MK, Giuntoli RL, Brown AJ. Importance and Timing of End-of-Life Care Discussions Among Gynecologic Oncology Patients. Am J Hosp Palliat Care 2012 Apr 24. PubMed PMID: 22531151. Epub 2012/04/26. Eng.

[5] Wright AA, Zhang B, Ray A, Mack JW, Trice E, Balboni T, et al. Associations between end-of-life discussions, patient mental health, medical care near death, and caregiver bereavement adjustment. *JAMA* 2008;300(14):1665-73.

[6] Hancock K, Clayton JM, Parker SM, Wal der S, Butow PN, Carrick S, et al. Truth-telling in discussing prognosis in advanced life-limiting illnesses: a systematic review. *Palliat Med* 2007;21(6):507-17.

[7] Quill TE. Perspectives on care at the close of life. Initiating end-of-life discussions with seriously ill patients: addressing the "elephant in the room". *JAMA* 2000;284(19):2502-7.

[8] Steinhauser KE, Christakis NA, Clipp EC, McNeilly M, Grambow S, Parker J, et al. Preparing for the end of life: preferences of patients, families, physicians, and other care providers. *J Pain Symptom Manage* 2001;22(3):727-37.

[9] Sahm S, Will R, Hommel G. What are cancer patients' preferences about treatment at the end of life, and who should start talking about it? A comparison with healthy people and medical staff. *Support Care Cancer* 2005;13(4):206-14.

[10] Hamel MB, Teno JM, Goldman L, Lynn J, Davis RB, Galanos AN, et al. Patient age and decisions to withhold life-sustaining treatments from seriously ill, hospitalized adults. SUPPORT Investigators. Study to Understand Prognoses and Preferences for Outcomes and Risks of Treatment. *Ann Intern Med* 1999;130(2):116-25.

[11] Hamel MB, Lynn J, Teno JM, Covinsky KE, Wu AW, Galanos A, et al. Age-related differences in care preferences, treatment decisions, and clinical outcomes of seriously ill hospitalized adults: lessons from SUPPORT. *J Am Geriatr Soc* 2000;48(5 Suppl):S176-82.

[12] Phillips RS, Wenger NS, Teno J, Oye RK, Youngner S, Califf R, et al. Choices of seriously ill patients about cardiopulmonary resuscitation: correlates and outcomes. SUPPORT Investigators. Study to Understand Prognoses and Preferences for Outcomes and Risks of Treatments. *Am J Med* 1996;100(2):128-37.

[13] Nilsson ME, Maciejewski PK, Zhang B, Wright AA, Trice ED, Muriel AC, et al. Mental health, treatment preferences, advance care planning, location, and quality of death in advanced cancer patients with dependent children. *Cancer* 2009;115(2):399-409.

[14] Hanchate A, Kronman AC, Young-Xu Y, Ash AS, Emanuel E. Racial and ethnic differences in end-of-life costs: why do minorities cost more than whites? *Arch Intern Med* 2009;169(5):493-501.

[15] Mack JW, Paulk ME, Viswanath K, Prigerson HG. Racial disparities in the outcomes of communication on medical care received near death. *Arch Intern Med* 2010;170(17):1533-40.

[16] Barnato AE, Anthony DL, Skinner J, Gallagher PM, Fisher ES. Racial and ethnic differences in preferences for end-of-life treatment. *J Gen Intern Med* 2009;24(6):695-701.

[17] Ano GG, Vasconcelles EB. Religious coping and psychological adjustment to stress: a meta-analysis. *J Clin Psychol* 2005;61(4):461-80.

[18] Canada AL, Parker PA, Basen-Engquist K, de Moor JS, Ramondetta LM. Active coping mediates the association between religion/spirituality and functional well-being in ovarian cancer. *Gynecol Oncol* 2005;99(3 Suppl 1):S125.

[19] Roberts JA, Brown D, Elkins T, Larson DB. Factors influencing views of patients with gynecologic cancer about end-of-life decisions. *Am J Obstet Gynecol* 1997;176(1 Pt 1):166-72.

[20] Phelps AC, Maciejewski PK, Nilsson M, Balboni TA, Wright AA, Paulk ME, et al. Religious coping and use of intensive life-prolonging care near death in patients with advanced cancer. *JAMA* 2009;301(11):1140-7.

[21] O'Connell LJ. Religious dimensions of dying and death. West J Med 1995;163(3):231-5.

[22] Ozanne EM, Partridge A, Moy B, Ellis KJ, Sepucha KR. Doctor-patient communication about advance directives in metastatic breast cancer. *J Palliat Med* 2009;12(6):547-53.

[23] Christakis NA, Lamont EB. Extent and determinants of error in doctors' prognoses in terminally ill patients: prospective cohort study. *BMJ* 2000;320(7233):469-72.

[24] Glare P, Virik K, Jones M, Hudson M, Eychmuller S, Simes J, et al. A systematic review of physicians' survival predictions in terminally ill cancer patients. *BMJ* 2003;327(7408):195-8.

In: Hospice Care
Editors: J. Hanl and S. Koeck

ISBN: 978-1-62618-456-5

Chapter 7

ETHICAL ISSUES IN HOSPICE

Padmashri Rastogi
Staff Physician, Dallas VA Medical Center, Department of Medicine,
UT Southwestern Medical Center, Dallas, TX, US

"To be with a person who is dying, to share consciousness with him, and to help him die consciously is one of the most exquisite manifestations of the Bodhisattva role."

Baba Ramdas

ABSTRACT

Hospice decreases the fear of dying alone, reduces the agony of death, and helps in maintaining dignity at the end of life. Hospice holds a special place in the care of dying patients. However, the tendency to avoid the topic of death as well as complex Medicare rules surround it still make hospice an enigma. Some of the ethical issues surrounding hospice are:

A .Should the referral to hospice be a prescription to abandon all hope?
B. Should a hospice patient have to forgo all acute care?
C. Can a patient with ongoing life sustaining treatment be referred to hospice?
D. Should a current DNR order be a requirement for enrollment in hospice?

E. Is palliative sedation acceptable for a hospice patient?
F. Is talking about death a must?
G. Is hospice care available only in institutions?
H. What is the role of artificial hydration and nutrition in a hospice patient?
I. How does one assess the decision-making capacity of a hospice patient?

In this chapter, we will clarify these ethical issues in hospice, proving that hospice is not only ethically sound, but a good care alternative in thwarting the pain of fast approaching death.

The word "hospice" comes from the Latin *hospitium* or hospitality, fitting as the concept originated with a disciple of Saint Jerome named Fabiola, who founded a facility in a Roman port to care for pilgrims returning from Africa. Not limited to only the dying, hospices continued to flourish throughout the Middle Ages as places of hospitality for the sick, the destitute, and the simple wayfarer. It was not until its modern incarnation that hospice became exclusively a place to provide comfort in the face of impending death [1].

This purpose was explicitly codified when hospice care was included in Medicare. Leon Panetta, a Democratic representative from California, sponsored legislation in 1980 and 1981 to include hospice in Medicare as a benefit for those with a terminal diagnoses in the last 6 months of life. Despite opposition from hospitals, nursing homes and home care agencies, the Senate passed the bill by unanimous vote on July 22, 1982. Current Medicare benefits for hospice care cover a variety of services with the goal of providing a good quality of life and control of symptoms when a patient with terminal illness has a life expectancy of 6 months or less.

Despite the current broad availability of hospice care, it remains greatly underutilized. It is estimated that only 20-50% of hospice-eligible advanced cancer patients are receiving hospice care at the time of death. Moreover, duration of hospice care is estimated at a mere six to eight weeks [2], suggesting that providers initiate and patients accept hospice care long after patients are eligible and barely in time for them to receive much benefit. While awareness and access to care could be barriers, it is clear that some explanations for both providers and patients' hesitancy to start hospice care must be found in the ethical dilemmas that surround hospice.

Hospice is viewed differently by the patient and the provider. The following case gives us a glimpse into the reasons behind the delay in referral to hospice. *Mrs. Smith, who was recently diagnosed with cholangiocarcinoma has a lot of faith in her oncologist and has hope that she may be cured. After several rounds of chemotherapy, today, her oncologist tells her that average survival for a patient like her is around 6 months. Further chemotherapy would be of no use, and he tells her all about hospice. She can stay home, and services will be provided at home. A hospice nurse will be in touch with her oncologist, and he will continue to provide advice. Mrs. Smith was not ready for this news, and she refuses to believe that no medication will work on her. She said she will go home and try to find a research protocol. A week later, Mrs. Smith made another appointment with the oncologist. Dr. Johnson listened to Mrs. Smith's concerns. He explained that by referring her to hospice, he was not giving up on her. In absence of active treatment, hospice would be the best program to control pain, provide symptomatic relief, and to provide compassionate care in her home without financial burden. The nurses will keep in touch with him and if she is not satisfied, she can always discontinue the hospice program. Mrs. Smith asked, "Isn't a hospice program all about death?" "No," said Dr. Johnson, "It's all about quality of life. We may not be able to change the quantity of life, but we can make sure you are comfortable, and hospice is the best program at this time."*

The first dilemma to consider is that which providers face before even bringing hospice care under consideration. A referral to hospice necessarily requires a terminal diagnosis, which is viewed as a prescription to abandon all hope. Thus, a physician who has no further curative therapy to offer a patient facing a terminal condition may still be unwilling to bring up hospice care because it would further rob the patient of hope. However, to not offer hospice care is to also rob the patient, this time of optimization of symptomatic relief and comfort care in the life remaining. Hospice care, then, should be viewed not as abandonment of therapy, but as pursuit of the best therapy at this point. Moreover, terminal prognosis can be communicated in such a way as to maintain hope. While a referral to hospice is based on a prognostication of life expectancy of 6 months or less, it is based on reasonable possibility and not certain knowledge [3].

Patients face concrete evidence of their grim prognosis in the process of enrolling in hospice, when they are asked to sign a DNR order, which states that the patient refuses Advanced Cardiac Life Support in the event of cardiopulmonary arrest. While DNR status is not a Medicare requirement for hospice care, it is imposed by many hospice care programs. The theoretical basis for DNR status of hospice patients lies in preventing futile resuscitation efforts in the face of a terminal illness. However, in practice, hospice patients with DNR orders live for a significantly shorter period of time than those without DNR orders, which likely reflects a failure to treat reversible illness in DNR patients. Indeed, the Triad III study showed that patients with a DNR status receive fewer resources and nursing care, even for reversible conditions. Thus, requiring DNR status for entry to hospice care creates the valid fear that one may succumb prematurely to reversible illness as opposed to the terminal disease [4].

Along with emergency resuscitation and active treatment for disease, it is a commonly encountered concept that hospice patients have to forgo all acute care as well. However, patients on hospice should be offered the same treatment for acute illness that is offered to patients not on hospice, although long term disease management may be different due to known limited life expectancy. Accordingly, Medicare covers this care for all Medicare eligible patients, including hospice patients. If acute illnesses like urosepsis or pneumonia are not diagnosed and treated promptly, a patient may suffer and/or die as a result, much sooner than from his hospice diagnosis. An argument can be made that acute infection may be better way of dying than a slow demise due to cachexia of cancer and double effect of pain medications. However, the purpose of hospice is not to give the patient a good death prematurely, but only to ensure quality of death when death is due. Thus, a hospice patient is entitled to go to the emergency room if there is a need [2]. For example, a hospice patient may develop hypercalcemia, causing significant distress, and treatment with hydration and bisphosphonates may provide relief. The only limitation is that hospice patients require referral to the ER through the hospice agency for coverage of hospital expenses by Medicare. Such hospitalizations do not only provide acute care but can also improve management of many issues in the hospice patients, and a study by Tang et. al. found that patients with acute care hospitalization during hospice survived longer than those hospice patients who had no hospitalization [5].

One gray area is related to ongoing life sustaining treatments for diseases other than one's terminal condition at the time patient enrolls in hospice. For example, a patient on hemodialysis may decide to be in hospice program for head and neck cancer. If one has to stop hemodialysis in order to enroll in hospice, the patient will suffer due to pulmonary edema, acidosis, and hyperkalemia and succumb to death in a matter of days, long before the patient will die of cancer. While such care should theoretically be allowed in keeping with the mission of hospice care, it is my personal observation that it is almost impossible to find a hospice agency which will allow patient to continue hemodialysis and enroll in hospice.

Pain control in hospice care also creates an ethical dilemma at times, as the use of high dose opioids has been questioned due to potential for adverse side effects especially sedation and respiratory depression [6]. Use has been justified by the doctrine of double effect (Pain medication is given for relief of pain but it may cause respiratory depression and death); however, it does not really apply as palliative sedation has not been shown to decrease overall survival [7]. Thus, if physical or emotional suffering due to pain cannot be controlled by usual dose of narcotics, palliative sedation can be used. Use does carry other side effects; Morita et al. found that high dose opioids impair the capability for complex communication from 43% at five days to 13% at one day prior to death [8].

Ethical issues in hospice involve not only the patient, but their family and caregivers as well. Caregiver stress is relatively decreased if hospice care is provided. The dilemma of the caregiver involves the delicate balance of how much to do for the family member. There may be concern that forcing nourishment and hydration can be perceived as extending life and prolonging suffering. At the same time,when giving higher doses of pain medication to keep the family member comfortable, they might be bothered by the thought of expediting death. Furthermore,there is always a concern of fast approaching death, particularly when the hospice patient develops new symptoms. Although the hospice services are available 24/7, many caregivers will be forced to call 911 so as not to delay care which can be life saving. This stress and uncertainitycan be reduced by making the family aware of the signs of impending death in a culturally appropriate manner. Morita et al. found in an observational study that these include radial pulselessness, respirations with mandibular movement, and cyanosis of fingers [9]. Others, like the development of a death rattle are highly predictive of death within 48 hours, but do not occur in all patients.

Lastly, as many patients will have waxing and waning level of consciousness due to their disease process, electrolyte abnormalities, and pain medications, it may be difficult to ascertain who has decision making capacity (DMC) and who does not. It would be best to assess the DMC in the earlier phases of disease and then discuss end of life issues. It should also be clarified whether patients would like to follow their instructions strictly or if surrogate decision makers can modify their instructions according to the circumstances. As much autonomy as practically possible should be given to the hospice patient.

Hospice has made significant changes in the last few years. The number of programs requiring DNR orders as admitting criteria have decreased. Debate about artificial hydration and nutrition has shifted away from mandatory requirements towards patients' autonomy. Controversy about high dose pain medication has been resolved in favor of prioritizing the patients' comfort rather than concern about the double effect. The education of caregivers has increased and they are now given written information about what to expect at the time near death. In addition, bereavement counseling is being started much sooner and continued until after death. Furthermore, the awareness of the availability of an ethics consult has increased which is helpful to resolve moral conflicts. Despite the moral debate, there are still myths to be dispelled regarding hospice care.

References

[1] Stoddard S: The Hospice movement : a better way of caring for the dying. New York, Stein and Day, 1978.

[2] Tang VL, French CJ, Cipher DJ, et al: Trends in Hospice Referral and Length of Stay at a Veterans Hospital Over the Past Decade. *Am. J. Hosp. Palliat Care,* 2012.

[3] Daugherty CK: Examining ethical dilemmas as obstacles to hospice and palliative care for advanced cancer patients. *Cancer Invest.,* 22:123-31, 2004.

[4] Mirarchi FL, Costello E, Puller J, et al: TRIAD III: nationwide assessment of living wills and do not resuscitate orders. *J. Emerg. Med.,* 42:511-20, 2012.

[5] Lamba S, Quest TE: Hospice care and the emergency department: rules, regulations, and referrals. *Ann. Emerg. Med.,* 57:282-90, 2011.

[6] Plonk WM, Jr., Arnold RM: Terminal care: the last weeks of life. *J. Palliat. Med.,*8:1042-54, 2005.

[7] Sykes N, Thorns A: Sedative use in the last week of life and the implications for end-of-life decision making. *Arch. Intern. Med.,* 163:341-4, 2003.

[8] Morita T, Hirai K, Akechi T, et al: Similarity and difference among standard medical care, palliative sedation therapy, and euthanasia: a multidimensional scaling analysis on physicians' and the general population's opinions. *J. Pain. Symptom. Manage.,*25:357-62, 2003.

[9] Morita T, Ichiki T, Tsunoda J, et al: A prospective study on the dying process in terminally ill cancer patients. Am. *J. Hosp. Palliat. Care,*15:217-22, 1998.

INDEX

A

abuse, 17
access, ix, 9, 82, 92, 104
accessibility, 46
accountability, 86
acetaminophen, 52
acidosis, 106
acquired immunodeficiency syndrome (AIDS), 10, 16
activism, 11
activity level, 68
acupuncture, 55
acute infection, 106
acute renal failure, 59
adjustment, 100, 101
adults, 16, 58, 59, 76, 77, 78, 100
advocacy, ix, 19, 21, 46, 89
affirming, 8, 20
Africa, 1, 104
African Americans, 96, 97
African-American, 59
age, 7, 54, 56, 86, 96, 100
agencies, 57, 86, 104
albumin, 48
alcohol use, 4
ALS, 63
ambivalence, 10
American culture, 83
American Psychological Association, 17
analgesic, 51, 58
anatomy, 89
aneurysm, 46
anger, 15
anxiety, ix, 4, 5, 6, 15, 61, 65, 70, 71
appetite, 5
arrest, 105
arthritis, 51
ascites, 46
assessment, 48, 54, 57, 62, 63, 68, 72, 73, 74, 75, 76, 78, 98, 108
atopic dermatitis, 58
atrial fibrillation, 46
attachment, 10
attachment theory, 10
attitudes, 6, 85, 91, 99
audit, 68, 73, 74
autonomy, 107
avoidance, 83
awareness, 12, 14, 104, 108

B

barriers, 3, 56, 104
base, 3
behaviors, 69, 85
benchmarks, 56
benefits, ix, 26, 46, 50, 55, 57, 81, 95, 104
benign, 97
bias, 7, 9, 12, 99

biomarkers, 48
biopsy, 46
BMI, 54
body weight, 54
bonds, 10
bowel, 46, 53
bowel obstruction, 46
breast cancer, 5, 16, 98, 101
breathing, ix, 61, 65, 70
breathlessness, 72

C

cachexia, 106
cancer, x, 4, 5, 16, 62, 63, 64, 65, 68, 77, 78, 84, 93, 94, 95, 97, 99, 100, 101, 104, 106, 108
cancer care, 4
carcinoma, 46, 76
caregivers, 95, 107, 108
category a, 63
Caucasians, 96, 97
CDC, 21
central nervous system (CNS), 52
certification, 63, 87
CFR, 73, 76
challenges, 4, 5, 7, 9, 10, 11, 13
chemotherapy, 46, 88, 105
Cheyne-Stokes respiration, 70
CHF, 46
children, 96, 101
cholangiocarcinoma, 104
cholecystitis, 46
cholecystostomy, 46
Christians, 18, 19, 20
chronic illness, 4
chronic kidney disease, 48, 51, 58
chronic obstructive pulmonary disease, 74, 84
citizens, 90
city, 61
CKD, 46, 47, 49, 50, 56, 57
classes, 89
clients, 17
climate, 2, 13
clinical judgment, 51, 85
clinical symptoms, 77
clothing, 66
collaboration, 68, 73, 85
communication, ix, x, 50, 56, 57, 65, 68, 73, 81, 83, 86, 94, 101, 107
communication skills, ix, 81, 86
community(ies), 6, 8, 11, 56, 57, 82, 86
comorbidity, 48
comparative analysis, viii
compilation, vii
compliance, ix, 61, 64, 65, 68, 73
complications, 56
conflict, 9
Congress, 46, 77
consciousness, 68, 103, 107
consensus, 49
contraceptives, 5
conversations, x, 93, 95, 97, 98
coordination, 83
COPD, 46, 64, 72, 74, 76, 77
coping strategies, ix, 62
copyright, 67
correlation, 54
cost, 24, 25, 50, 54, 90, 91, 101
counsel, 83
counseling, 17, 108
creatinine, 54
CT, 20
culture, 15, 18, 86
cure, 98
curricula, 84, 88, 90
curriculum, ix, 81, 84, 89, 90, 91
cyanosis, 107

D

data collection, ix, 61, 63, 64, 74
deaths, 47, 51, 58
decision makers, 107
decision-making process, 47, 56
dementia, 62, 63, 64, 66, 74, 75, 76, 77, 78, 84
denial, 74
depression, viii, 4, 5, 7, 9, 45, 57, 75, 107

dialysis, viii, 45, 46, 47, 48, 49, 50, 51, 53, 54, 55, 56, 57, 58, 59, 96
diastolic function, 46
digestion, 54
dignity, ix, x, 46, 82, 83, 103
directives, ix, 81, 95, 96, 98, 101
disability, 56
disclosure, 16
discomfort, 51, 98
discrimination, 2, 4, 5, 9, 10, 11
disease progression, 48
diseases, 4, 56, 58, 66, 98, 106
dissonance, 18
distress, ix, 6, 17, 53, 81, 99, 106
distribution, 53
diversity, viii, 2, 17
DNR order, x, 96, 103, 105, 107
doctors, 88, 89, 101
dosing, 51, 52
double-blind trial, 58
draft, 65
drugs, 4, 52, 55, 96
dyspnea, 72, 76

E

echocardiogram, 46
education, ix, 48, 56, 81, 83, 84, 87, 88, 89, 90, 108
educational experience, 85
educational process, 87
elders, 21
electrolyte, 107
eligibility criteria, ix, 61
e-mail, 93
emergency, 89, 106, 108
emotional distress, 95
emotional state, 76
end of life care, ix, 15, 68, 82
endometriosis, 5
end-stage renal disease, 58, 59
enemas, 53
energy, viii, 45, 54, 57
England, 8, 15
enrollment, x, 56, 96, 103
environment(s), 3, 9, 13, 24, 95
equality, 6, 12
ESRD, viii, 45, 46, 47, 48, 49, 50, 51, 52, 53, 54, 55, 56, 57, 58
ethical issues, vii, x, 103, 104
ethics, 84, 88, 108
Europe, viii, 1
euthanasia, 55, 108
evidence, vii, viii, ix, 2, 3, 11, 14, 18, 52, 61, 62, 65, 67, 68, 72, 85, 86, 90, 91, 105
excitability, 53
exclusion, 7, 8
excretion, 55
exertion, 75
expenditures, 62
expertise, 54, 56
exposure, 5, 9, 99

F

faith, 8, 18, 20, 104
families, ix, 9, 10, 11, 12, 47, 48, 50, 56, 59, 81, 85, 86, 90, 94, 100
family members, 53, 83
fear(s), x, 7, 14, 95, 98, 103, 106
Federal Register, 63, 76
federal regulations, 64
feelings, 14
financial, 9, 105
financial resources, 9
Finland, v, vii, viii, 25, 26
flexibility, 56
fluid, 55
formation, 10, 11, 97
fractures, 83
friendship, 10
funding, 87
funds, viii, 45, 88

G

gallbladder, 46
gay men, 4, 8, 15, 17, 18, 19, 20
gender identity, 11, 14

general practitioner, 17
goal attainment, 99
God, 46
Great Britain, 20
growth, 87, 97
guidance, 55, 64, 94, 97
guidelines, vii, viii, ix, 2, 3, 7, 12, 13, 45, 48, 49, 50, 51, 56, 57, 58, 59, 61, 63, 68, 78, 97, 99
gynecologic oncologist, x, 93, 94

H

half-life, 52, 55
harassment, 6
head and neck cancer, 106
healing, 83
health, vii, 2, 3, 4, 5, 6, 7, 8, 9, 10, 11, 12, 13, 15, 16, 17, 18, 19, 46, 58, 59, 68, 71, 76, 82, 83, 85, 86, 88, 89, 90, 91, 94, 96, 101
health care, 3, 4, 7, 15, 16, 19, 59, 68, 76, 82, 83, 85, 86, 88, 89, 90, 91, 94
health care professionals, 7, 83, 85
health care system, 90
health problems, 6, 19
health risks, 6
health sciences, vii, 2
health services, vii, 6, 7, 9, 18
healthcare needs, vii, 1, 3, 4
healthcare providers, vii, 1, 3, 4, 6, 9, 10, 11, 13, 47, 48, 56, 57
heart disease, 62, 63, 74
heart failure, 84
hemodialysis, 46, 47, 51, 53, 55, 56, 58, 106
hepatotoxicity, 52
hermeneutics, 20
heterosexuality, 6, 14
heterosexuals, 4
Hispanics, 96, 97
history, 56
HIV, 17, 63
hobby, 67
homosexuality, 9, 12
hospice, vii, viii, ix, x, 2, 3, 4, 5, 6, 7, 9, 10, 12, 13, 14, 46, 56, 57, 59, 61, 62, 63, 64, 65, 66, 68, 72, 73, 74, 75, 76, 78, 82, 84, 85, 86, 87, 89, 90, 91, 92, 95, 96, 103, 104, 105, 106, 107, 108
hospice patients, vii, 63, 65, 72, 105, 106
hospital death, 96
hospitality, 104
hospitalization, 64, 106
hostility, 10
human, 2, 5, 13, 16, 17
human immunodeficiency virus, 16
human papilloma virus (HPV), 5, 17
human right, 2, 13
human rights, 2, 13
Hunter, 16
hypercalcemia, 106
hyperkalemia, 106
hyperparathyroidism, 54
hypertension, 74
hyperventilation, 70

I

iatrogenic, 52, 54
ideal, 49
identity, 8, 13, 16, 19
Impact Assessment, 11
improvements, 55, 73, 88, 96
incidence, 5, 97
individuals, 8, 14, 18, 19, 70
inequality, 11
infection, 16, 17
initiation, 49, 50, 58, 59, 98
injury, 47
insomnia, 5
institutions, x, 104
insulin, 54
insulin resistance, 54
integration, x, 19, 94
intensive care unit, 89, 91
intermediaries, ix, 61, 62
interpersonal relations, 86
interpersonal relationships, 86
intervention, 55

intimacy, 15
investment, 50
Iowa, 78
Ireland, vii, 1, 2, 3, 7, 9, 11, 12, 13
isolation, 9
issues, vii, x, 2, 3, 4, 7, 8, 12, 13, 15, 17, 18, 20, 89, 96, 99, 106, 107

K

kidney, 47, 48, 49, 51, 55, 56, 57, 58, 59
kidney failure, 47

L

later life, 4, 15
lead, 3, 5, 9, 52, 54, 98
legal issues, vii, 2
legislation, 3, 9, 11, 12, 104
lesions, 5
life expectancy, 50, 75, 95, 104, 105, 106
life experiences, 10, 11
lifetime, 5
light, 99
liver, 52, 63
liver disease, 63
loans, 87
longevity, 47

M

majority, 95
malignancy, 94
malnutrition, viii, 45, 54, 57
man, 14, 46
management, vii, ix, x, 20, 25, 46, 51, 55, 57, 72, 73, 81, 83, 90, 93, 94, 99, 106
marginalisation, 5, 10, 11
marginalization, 3, 4, 11
marketing, 66
marriage, 2, 9
mass, ix, 81, 90, 91
materials, 12
matter, 56, 106
measurement(s), 63, 65, 68, 69, 73, 76
mechanical ventilation, 96, 97
median, 95
Medicaid, 63, 64, 88
medical, ix, x, 12, 25, 47, 48, 50, 55, 56, 65, 73, 81, 82, 83, 84, 86, 87, 88, 89, 90, 91, 93, 94, 95, 96, 99, 100, 101, 108
medical care, 83, 84, 88, 89, 95, 99, 100, 101, 108
Medicare, viii, ix, x, 45, 47, 61, 62, 63, 64, 65, 68, 74, 77, 78, 82, 84, 88, 89, 90, 97, 103, 104, 105, 106
medication, 52, 53, 105, 107, 108
medicine, vii, ix, 15, 56, 81, 82, 83, 84, 85, 86, 87, 88, 89, 90, 91
mental health, 4, 6, 7, 13, 17, 18, 96, 100
mental illness, 4, 20
meta-analysis, 101
metabolic acidosis, 54
metabolites, 52, 53, 54, 55
metabolized, 52
minorities, 6, 17, 96, 101
minority groups, 6
miscommunication, 96
mission, 106
misunderstanding, 89
models, vii, 2, 5, 10
morbidity, 48, 50, 58
morphine, 52, 53, 54
mortality, viii, 45, 47, 48, 58
mortality rate, viii, 45, 47
Moses, 77
multidimensional, 108
muscle mass, 54
music, 65, 68
Muslims, 20

N

narcotics, 107
narratives, 20
National Health Service (NHS), , ix, 11, 21, 82, 89
National Institutes of Health, 59
negative effects, 6

negative experiences, 4, 9, 12
negative relation, 8
nephrologist, 46
nervous system, 52
Netherlands, 58
neuropathic pain, 53
neuropathy, viii, 45, 57
neutral, 56
New Zealand, 19, 49
NHANES, 54
nitrogen, 76
Norway, 24
nurses, 7, 17, 68, 73, 105
nursing, 12, 50, 68, 72, 74, 77, 104, 106
nursing care, 106
nursing home, 50, 77, 104
nutrition, x, 54, 104, 107
nutritional status, 54

O

Obama, 89
obesity, 4
obstacles, 108
OCS, 76
oncologist, 46, 104
opiates, 53
opioids, 52, 106
optimization, 105
ovarian cancer, 101
overweight, 5
oxygen, 74

P

pacing, 70
pain, viii, ix, x, 45, 51, 52, 53, 55, 57, 58, 61, 63, 64, 65, 68, 69, 70, 74, 75, 76, 77, 78, 82, 98, 104, 105, 106, 107
pain management, viii, 45, 51, 52, 64, 68, 82
palliative, vii, viii, ix, x, 1, 2, 3, 5, 6, 7, 8, 9, 11, 12, 13, 17, 25, 45, 48, 51, 56, 57, 58, 68, 75, 76, 78, 81, 82, 83, 84, 85, 86, 87, 88, 89, 90, 91, 103, 107, 108
palliative care, viii, ix, 2, 5, 6, 7, 8, 9, 11, 12, 14, 17, 25, 48, 57, 58, 75, 78, 81, 82, 84, 85, 86, 87, 88, 90, 91, 108
panic attack, 5
parenting, 7
participants, 12, 13, 19
pathophysiology, 89
patient care, 56, 63, 65, 82, 86, 90, 91
peer review, 1
peritonitis, 46
permission, 67
physical activity, 74
physical health, 3
physicians, ix, x, 15, 47, 51, 56, 81, 82, 84, 86, 87, 88, 89, 90, 94, 95, 97, 98, 99, 100, 101, 108
physiology, 57
placebo, 58, 59
PNA, 54
pneumonia, 106
policy, viii, ix, 11, 12, 18, 45, 47, 81, 82, 84, 87, 88
policy options, ix, 81
policymakers, 88
population, viii, 3, 8, 16, 20, 45, 47, 49, 51, 52, 57, 64, 69, 70, 85, 86, 95, 108
praxis, 88
prayer, 8, 71
pregnancy, 5
prejudice, 2, 6
preparation, 83
President Obama, 82, 89
primary caregivers, 10
principles, 47, 57, 84, 86, 89, 90
probability, 46, 91
problem-based learning, 89
problem-solving, 74
professional development, 13, 86
professionals, ix, 2, 4, 12, 14, 55, 56, 59, 81, 82, 86, 88, 99
profit, 62, 64, 84
profit margin, 62

prognosis, ix, 26, 46, 50, 56, 57, 66, 70, 77, 94, 95, 100, 105
project, 14, 19, 85
prophylactic, 54
prostate cancer, 74
pruritus, 58, 59
psychological distress, 6
psychological health, 18
psychology, 10, 16
psychosocial support, 90
psychotherapy, 17, 19
public health, viii, 45, 56, 85
public policy, 84
pulmonary edema, 106
pulmonary hypertension, 46

Q

quality of life, viii, ix, 45, 47, 49, 50, 51, 56, 57, 58, 61, 62, 64, 84, 85, 86, 90, 91, 94, 95, 104, 105
quality standards, 50
questioning, 18, 86

R

race, 4, 96
rating scale, 68, 73, 75, 78
reactions, 6
recommendations, viii, 2, 50
recovery, 83
reform, ix, 82, 83, 89
regulations, 63, 108
regulatory requirements, 62, 65, 74
rehabilitation, 74
rejection, 9
relevance, 7, 89
reliability, 72, 78
relief, 51, 82, 105, 106, 107
religion, 8, 9, 20, 96, 97, 101
religious beliefs, 20
renal failure, 46, 52, 55
replication, 76
reputation, viii
requirements, ix, 61, 63, 64, 65, 68, 69, 73, 74, 81, 87, 107
researchers, 8, 9
reserves, 50
resilience, 7, 10, 11, 16
resolution, 18
resource allocation, 25
resources, 7, 48, 57, 73, 82, 83, 86, 106
respiratory failure, 64
response, 7, 62
responsiveness, 86
rights, 2, 13
risk(s), ix, 4, 6, 7, 16, 17, 46, 47, 54, 55, 57, 95
risk factors, 4, 7, 16, 17
rules, x, 103, 108

S

safety, 10, 52, 64
scaling, 108
Scandinavia, viii
school, ix, 6, 11, 81, 84, 86, 88, 89, 90
science, 85, 89
self-esteem, 98
self-interest, 86
self-reflection, 86
Senate, 104
sensitivity, 3, 7, 14, 86
services, viii, 3, 7, 12, 13, 19, 45, 57, 66, 74, 82, 88, 96, 104, 105, 107
sex, 2, 3, 5, 9, 10, 14, 17, 21
sexual health, 17
sexual orientation, 4, 8, 11, 13, 15
sexuality, 2, 11, 20
shame, 9
shortage, 87
shortness of breath, 72
side effects, 107
signs, 107
social care, 12
social change, 11
social context, 5
social exclusion, 6
social network, 4

social sciences, 85
social stress, 18
social support, 57
social welfare, 26
social withdrawal, 5
social workers, 12, 65, 68, 73
society, 9, 11, 16, 86
South Africa, 1
specialists, 48, 55, 56, 57, 82, 87
specific knowledge, 85
speech, 70
spiritual care, 65, 68, 71, 72, 73
spiritual needs, ix, 81, 82
spirituality, 11, 16, 97, 101
stakeholders, 13
state(s), ix, 5, 7, 64, 81, 87, 95, 105
stigma, 6, 90
stress, 3, 5, 6, 7, 8, 10, 18, 50, 94, 95, 101, 107
stressors, 6
stroke, 63
structure, 76
substance use, 4
suicidal ideation, 4, 9
suicide, 10, 82
support staff, 73
survival, 4, 46, 48, 49, 58, 68, 77, 78, 101, 105, 107
Sweden, 24
symptomology, 6
symptoms, 5, 49, 50, 55, 57, 58, 65, 74, 104, 107

T

Task Force, 4, 47, 56
teams, vii, 2, 50, 86
techniques, 48, 55, 74
technology(ies), ix, 46, 82, 83
terminal illness, 99, 104, 105
terminal patients, 84, 87, 94
terminally ill, x, 77, 82, 83, 87, 93, 95, 101, 108
therapeutic interventions, 85
therapy, viii, 45, 46, 47, 49, 55, 57, 58, 105, 108
thoughts, 95
tissue, 66
tobacco, 4
toxicity, 51, 52
trainees, 56, 84, 85
training, vii, ix, 1, 3, 5, 6, 7, 11, 12, 13, 14, 25, 56, 58, 81, 82, 83, 84, 85, 87, 88, 89, 90, 98
training programs, ix, 56, 81, 87, 89
trajectory, 67, 68, 70, 72
transgender, vii, 1, 2, 3, 6, 14, 15, 16, 17, 18, 19, 20, 21
transplant, 55
treatment, viii, x, 17, 45, 50, 55, 56, 57, 58, 59, 76, 84, 92, 93, 94, 96, 98, 99, 100, 101, 103, 105, 106
trial, 58, 59
tumor, 46

U

uniform, viii, 62, 87
unions, 2, 9
United Kingdom (UK), 3, 8, 11, 20, 24
United Nations, 13
United States, v, vii, viii, ix, 45, 47, 56, 59, 81, 82, 83, 84, 85, 89, 90, 91, 94
urban, 4
urban areas, 4
uremic pruritis, viii, 45, 57
urine, 52
usual dose, 107

V

validation, 77
variations, 70
victimization, 6
violence, 9
vote, 104
vulnerability, 74

W

Washington, 17, 76, 77, 78, 91
water, 66
wear, 66
web, 67
welfare, viii, 26
welfare state, viii, 26
well-being, 2, 5, 10, 13, 18, 85, 101
withdrawal, 49, 55, 59
workers, 14, 66
workforce, 46, 82
World Health Organization (WHO), 51

Y

yield, 91
young adults, 47
young people, 4, 18